T0044259

MORE BY EUGENE H. PETERSON
FROM WATERBROOK

*This Hallelujah Banquet: How the End of
What We Were Reveals Who We Can Be*

*As Kingfishers Catch Fire: A Conversation on
the Ways of God Formed by the Words of God*

*Every Step an Arrival: A 90-Day Devotional
for Exploring God's Word*

*A Month of Sundays: Thirty-One Days of
Wrestling with Matthew, Mark, Luke, and John*

BY WINN COLLIER

*A Burning in My Bones: The Authorized Biography of
Eugene H. Peterson, Translator of The Message*

congregation—matters so much. These pages are not pious abstractions but personal words to friends, inviting all of us to embrace God's enchanting invitation to truly live."

—WINN COLLIER, director of the Eugene Peterson Center for Christian Imagination at Western Theological Seminary and author of *Love Big, Be Well* and *A Burning in My Bones*

"Wisdom literature in the biblical tradition helps us discern the good life as God intends it. Here we have a collection of Eugene Peterson's pastoral wisdom, reflections on the Scriptures, and meditations on the life and way of Jesus. These words carry the tenderness of Peterson's voice and the keenness of his insight. Here is fertilizer for our formation and flourishing in the Jesus kind of life."

—REV. GLENN PACKIAM, associate senior pastor of New Life Church and author of *Blessed Broken Given*

"We don't hear the word *sage* much anymore because there are so few sages these days. But Eugene Peterson was one of deep wisdom. In an age awash in banal how-to books, *On Living Well* is something else entirely—something we need. *On Living Well* is a series of meditations on what constitutes the good life, written by a man who indeed knew how to live well. This book brims with the wisdom our day needs."

—BRIAN ZAHND, pastor of Word of Life Church and author of *When Everything's on Fire*

"Eugene insisted that the crux of Christian spirituality was to get all these God-truths lived, to get them moving into the street. God's wisdom, Eugene knew, is always relational, always drawing us into the questions, complications, dangers, and joys of genuine life pursued before God and alongside one another. This is why the context of much that we read here—pastoral words written to Eugene's small

PRAISE FOR

On Living Well

"Eugene Peterson is a voice that keeps pulling me back to where I was created to be. Through his insights, stories, and sermons, his words woo the weary soul into the comfort of God's presence and power. *On Living Well* is calming, encouraging, and profound."

—MATT CHANDLER, lead pastor
of the Village Church

"Among the many gifts of human language, the greatest is the use of words for the worship of God, who is the Word. On these pages, over and over, Peterson's words raise our sense of God's sheer worthiness out of the clutter of confusion and complication. The simplicity and strength of language in *On Living Well* is seldom found but should be greatly treasured. These words are pure acts of worship that will bring the reader into beautiful worship of the source of all beauty."

—KAREN SWALLOW PRIOR, research professor
of English, as well as Christianity and Culture,
at Southeastern Baptist Theological Seminary
and author of *On Reading Well*

On Living Well

On Living Well

Brief Reflections
on Wisdom for Walking
in the Way of Jesus

EUGENE H. PETERSON

WATERBROOK

On Living Well

All Scripture quotations, unless otherwise indicated, are taken from the New Revised Standard Version Bible, copyright © 1989 National Council of the Churches of Christ in the United States of America. Used by permission. All rights reserved worldwide. Scripture quotations marked (MSG) are taken from The Message. Copyright © 1993, 2002, 2018 by Eugene H. Peterson. Used by permission of NavPress. All rights reserved. Represented by Tyndale House Publishers, a division of Tyndale House Ministries. Scripture quotations marked (PHILLIPS) are taken from the New Testament in Modern English by J. B. Phillips, copyright © 1960, 1972 J. B. Phillips. Administered by the Archbishops' Council of the Church of England. Used by Permission. Scripture quotations marked (RSV) are taken from the Revised Standard Version of the Bible, copyright © 1946, 1952, and 1971 National Council of the Churches of Christ in the United States of America. Used by permission. All rights reserved worldwide.

Copyright © 2021 by Eugene H. Peterson

All rights reserved.

Published in the United States by WaterBrook, an imprint of Random House, a division of Penguin Random House LLC.

WATERBROOK® and its deer colophon are registered trademarks of Penguin Random House LLC.

LIBRARY OF CONGRESS CATALOGING-IN-PUBLICATION DATA
Names: Peterson, Eugene H., 1932–2018, author.
Title: On living well : brief reflections on wisdom for walking in the way of Jesus / Eugene H. Peterson.
Description: First edition. | Colorado Springs : WaterBrook, [2021] | Includes bibliographical references.
Identifiers: LCCN 2021017532 | ISBN 9781601429797 (hardcover) | ISBN 9781601429803 (ebook)
Subjects: LCSH: Christian life—Meditations.
Classification: LCC BV4501.3 .P47525 2021 | DDC 248.4—dc23
LC record available at https://lccn.loc.gov/2021017532

Printed in Canada on acid-free paper

waterbrookmultnomah.com

2 4 6 8 9 7 5 3 1

First Edition

Images on title page and part-title pages: copyright © iStock.com/funnybank

Book design by Victoria Wong

SPECIAL SALES Most WaterBrook books are available at special quantity discounts when purchased in bulk by corporations, organizations, and special-interest groups. Custom imprinting or excerpting can also be done to fit special needs. For information, please email specialmarketscms@penguinrandomhouse.com.

Start with GOD—the first step in learning is
   bowing down to GOD;
only fools thumb their noses at such wisdom.

Proverbs 1:7, MSG

Foreword

I remember exactly where I was when I first came across a book by Eugene Peterson. It was the spring of 2006 in downtown Brooklyn. I was on my lunch break, doing what was an almost-daily practice then—haunting the local bookstore. I walked up and down the aisles, looking to spend money I *really* didn't have, being the twenty-six-year-old pastor I was. That day, I encountered a title that intrigued me: *Christ Plays in Ten Thousand Places*.

What an odd title, I thought. The author's name was vaguely familiar (I did own *The Message* but didn't know it was Eugene's work). I picked up the book and opened it—with just five minutes remaining on my lunch break—and started reading.

Twenty minutes later, I found myself engrossed in Eugene's delightful prose and penetrating theological insights, not realizing how much time had elapsed. Frantically, I hid the copy—the last one remaining—in a different section of the store. When lunchtime came the following day, I ran out of the office, remembering exactly where I had placed the book. I bought it and soon had marked up almost every page. A soul was growing in Brooklyn. Since that moment, this has been my story with Eugene: if he wrote it, I read it.

Along the way, Eugene's incisive words and penchant for

integrating insights from often-overlooked or compartmentalized spaces have profoundly shaped me. In many ways, Eugene's work was my "gateway drug." New vistas of theological insight and literature began to open to me. (I read novels and poetry today in large part because of him.) Through his witness, I was confronted with a refreshing burden for holy preaching flowing out of the unforced rhythms of grace.

His all-consuming commitment to Christ, the Scriptures, and the church's witness in the world gave me a vision for the kind of faith and pastoral imagination I knew God called me to—one that named and resisted the idols of efficiency, anxious power plays, and superficial discipleship metrics. It's a vision I continue to strive toward.

We desperately need the emphases of Eugene's spiritual formation today. We need new calls to *presence* with God, fresh encounters with the One who meets us in the biblical narrative, and a radical practice of discernment amid the noise and values of our culture. In short, we need training on how to live well—instruction for a long obedience. *Wisdom*. My heart's cry is to live in this manner: wisely plumbing the depths of God's countercultural ways, with full confidence that love, joy, and peace are realities the Spirit graciously leads us into.

The book you are holding offers a path toward that end. I've been reading Eugene for over fifteen years, yet in this book I was once again struck by his love for words and the beautiful distillation of wisdom in them. In this book, Eugene covers a wide array of themes we desperately need formation around, all aiming toward an everyday life lived well.

To live well is not about achievements, possessions, or comfort. Those words are far too superficial. Living well is about congruence, integrity, and, most importantly, love. Living well flows out of a commitment to interiority—examining the movements of the heart in full recognition that God comes to us in those spaces. To live well is to embrace our "embodiedness," which helps us savor the sacred in all we do, whether at work, play, or rest. Living well is revealed in our ability to be present to the presence of God and the presence of others. Living well emerges out of contemplation, nuanced thinking, relaxed dialogue, long naps, and certainly good wine. If there's anything the world needs, it's wisdom on living well. The reflections in this book offer just that.

As you read this book, pay close attention to the invitations God will offer you. There is something here for everyone—whether you are a pastor, a new believer, or simply someone searching for the divine. Some of the sections, short though they are, require a kind of *Lectio Divina* (i.e., an unhurried, repetitive, prayerful reading) to access the depth of wisdom before us. As Eugene faithfully modeled, a life lived well is unthinkable if we are skimming, rushing, and cutting corners. Consider reading this with a journal nearby, ready to chew on the truth being served to you. And, of course, utilize this book as a springboard for prayer, because the words you will encounter here are not just about new information but are for our formation in Christ.

—RICH VILLODAS
New York City, 2021

Contents

Part Three: On Prayers and Praises

Part Five: On Glories

Editor's Note

Eugene H. Peterson believed in the extraordinary spirituality of ordinary life. Rather than drawing us away from the earthy, rough edges of living, he urged Christians to become more human, not less so, as they grew in the life of Jesus. Everyday existence is a place of great beauty, real danger, and frequent humor, and walking in wisdom is the trick to navigating the complexities the world has put in our path. To encourage this walk of Christian wisdom, Eugene pastored, preached, taught, wrote, and, most of all, *lived.*

Among Eugene's extensive archives and unpublished resources are countless examples of the beautiful, earthy wisdom born from this vision of life in Jesus. Many of them are very brief—an aside here, a parenthetical statement there—but, in the tradition of great spiritual writing, *deep.* They come from an earned and rooted wisdom, all carrying a keen point: to help others walk in the way of Jesus with a little more faithfulness, skill, and understanding.

On Living Well collects many of the best of these gems. Much of the material here was drawn from more than two decades of *Amen!,* a weekly letter Eugene circulated to his beloved members of Christ Our King Presbyterian Church in Bel Air, Maryland. The quality and depth of the short pastoral writing that Eugene included in nearly every edition of that newsletter is a remarkable testament to his craft as a writer and his commitment to excellence in even the smallest opportunities. Other material was taken from sermons preached at Christ Our King during the same period or from other short, unpublished writings he produced as a working pastor. Our editing has been very limited: we've updated some dated cultural references, made various small additions or subtractions for clarity and crispness of language, and then organized them into a meaningful whole. While readers are encouraged to encounter these short sections in any order (or no order at all), readers who do choose to move from the first page to the last will be rewarded with, we hope, a sense of crafted cohesion and a natural flow in which Eugene would have delighted.

The wisdom in this book represents Eugene at the height of his pastoral work, speaking with candor, warmth, and directness to those under his care. It is the hope of the WaterBrook team, in close partnership with Eugene's family, that you will feel yourself pastored from beyond the limitations of years by his timeless biblical insight and keen love for the wonders of the Christian life in the real world. Yes, our world.

Live well.

—PAUL J. PASTOR, editor

Introduction

We've never done this before—*lived*, that is. We are novices at life, having to learn as we go. The animals have instincts that carry them pretty well through their life spans; we have to learn it all firsthand. But it doesn't have to be all trial and error.

We can take note of men and women who have done this well and keep company with them. We can see how they have done it, hoping to get the hang of it ourselves so that we will live well, live completely, live in great love with the people around us, and live in great faith in God.

We can look for lives worth watching. We can look for those who did this well, who lived in love and lived in faith. We can look for those who leave little unlived life around them, who can show us what is possible for ourselves, and who can whet our appetites for the best—the human best.

The Christ best.

PART ONE

On Beginnings

Forget about what's happened;
  don't keep going over old history.
Be alert, be present. I'm about to do
  something brand-new.
  It's bursting out! Don't you see it?
There it is! I'm making a road
  through the desert,
  rivers in the badlands.

Isaiah 43:18–19, MSG

The Word Was First

Before I formed you in the womb I knew you,
and before you were born I consecrated you;
I appointed you a prophet to the nations.

Jeremiah 1:5

The Word was first. The Word was previous to everything else. Before we were conceived and took shape in our mothers' wombs, before we were born, before anything happened, there was the Word.

Before there was a sun or a moon or stars, there was the Word. Before there were trees and flowers and fish, there was the Word. Before there were governments and hospitals and schools, there was the Word.

If the Word were not first, everything would have gone awry. If the Word were second—or third or fourth—we would have lost touch with the deep, divine rhythms of creation. If the Word were pushed out of the way and made to be a servant to the action and program, we would have lost connection with the vast interior springs of redemption that flow out of our Lord, the Word made flesh.

When the Word is treated casually or carelessly, we wander away from the essential personal intimacies that God creates . . . by his Word.

On Birth

Every birth is a wonder. The world is invaded by life. Space and time are penetrated by being. Emptiness is displaced by shape and movement. Silence is filled with tone and melody. Solitude becomes society. A birth produces tremors and shakes us in the depths of our person, moving our very universe.

Uncalculated energies are released; unpredictable creations are formed. We are moved by those energies, changed by them, and loosed from death and plunged into life by them. Birth is both a physical experience and a faith event.

Our first birth thrusts us kicking and squalling into the light of day. Our second birth places us singing and believing in the light of God. By acts of love previous to us, we are launched into ways of seeing and being that become truly ours. We are launched into *life*.

Though an everyday reality, birth is always awesome, whether as a new baby in the world or as a new creature in Christ.

We Are Not Stuck

D istracted, inconstant people like us need a large attention-getting device for noticing the main show, seeing the huge God-dimensions of our lives, and listening to the large God-story into which all our stories fit.

There is much about those stories that we, of course, cannot change. We cannot change our heights or our ages. We cannot change our basic intelligences. We cannot change our places of birth or our parentages. We can, at best, make modifications on only our bodily shapes and emotional temperaments. There is a great deal of sheer *givenness* in our lives, circumstances, and conditions that we must deal with as it is.

Frequently, we project fantasies of what we want onto the church and then walk away grumpy because we don't find what we expect. Other times, we become paralyzed with guilt because we feel the church isn't living up to its calling, but all our guilt does is drain more energy out of us. What we simply must do is attend to what is going on—this Holy Spirit work that is continuous between the Acts of the Apostles and the acts of the Christians of our community, here in our place, now in our time.

But still, we are not stuck with these lives of ours the way they are. We can change—can *be* changed. That is the promise of God in Jesus Christ and the experience that is at the heart of Christian living: *conversion.*

What this means is simple. At the center, at the core of our beings, change is possible. A change from being lost to found, a change from self-centeredness to God-centeredness, a change from anxiously grasping to confidently receiving the life of faith in Jesus Christ.

These changes are going on all around us. Sometimes they are taking place in us. An American view of conversion sees it as characteristically sudden and dramatic, and if it isn't sudden and dramatic, then it doesn't qualify. But most conversions are long and quiet. We miss the drama of these stories because we are not sufficiently trained biblically to discern Spirit work.

You don't have to stay the way you are.

On Growing

> Then Jesus was led up by the Spirit into the wilderness to be tempted by the devil. He fasted forty days and forty nights, and afterwards he was famished.
>
> Matthew 4:1–2

It is hard to be a human being. Of all the creatures in this world, we have the toughest task. It is easy to be a crocus: no decisions to make, no schedules to keep, and no disappointments to endure. The crocus sleeps all winter, and then as the snow recedes and the sun warms the earth, the crocus breaks through the ground with blossoms that bring standing applause from all of us. It is easy to be a cat: no anxieties about aging, no perplexities about world affairs, and no guilt about real or imagined adulteries. The cat grooms itself on the carpet, purrs on any convenient lap, and holds the opinions of the servile humans in haughty disdain.

But being human is not easy. Not at *all* easy. The seasons do not automatically develop us into maturity. Our instincts do not naturally guide us into a superior contentment. We falter and fail. We doubt and question. We work and learn. And just when we think we have it figured out, something else comes up that throws us for a loop.

Jesus is the best look we have at what it means to be human—*really* human. We look at him and see the incredible attractiveness and profound wonder of being a woman or a man. We also see how difficult it is. We see him in contest against every force that would diminish us into something less than human. We see him confront and deal with every influence that would divert us from living to the glory of God.

We get our basic orientation in the difficulties of being human by carefully attending to what Jesus said and did in his forty days of temptation and testing in the wilderness. To become like him, we must be changed, shaped, and deepened by the Word of God.

Fresh Salt

Remember the words of our Lord when he said, "Salt is good; but if salt has lost its taste, how can its saltiness be restored?" (Luke 14:34).

The answer to his question is simple.

It can't.

You have to go back to the salt mines. You have to dig some fresh salt.

Saints, Not Cogwheels

For a long time, all Christians called each other saints. They were all saints regardless of how well or badly they lived, of how experienced or inexperienced they were. The word *saint* did not refer to the quality or virtue of their acts but rather to the kind of life to which they had been chosen: life on a battlefield. It was not a title given after a spectacular performance; it was a mark of whose side they were on.

Saint means being set apart for God's side. That word means that a human is not a cogwheel. It means that a person is not the keyboard of a piano on which circumstances play hit tunes or parade music. It means we are chosen out of the stream of circumstantiality for something important that God is doing.

What is God doing? He is doing what he has always done. He is saving. He is rescuing. He is blessing. He is providing. He is judging. He is healing. He is enlightening. There is a spiritual war in progress in our world, an all-out moral battle. There is evil and cruelty, unhappiness and illness. There is superstition and ignorance, brutality and pain. God is in a continuous and an energetic battle against all of it.

God is for life and against death. God is for love and against hate. God is for hope and against despair. God is for heaven and against hell. There is no neutral ground in the universe. Every square foot of space is contested.

And every one of us is enlisted on his side in the contest.

An Unanswered Question

What gets our attention? We are bombarded with ideas, invitations, arguments, and enthusiasms that claim to make us better or happy or safe. We are yelled at, bartered with, urged, and pushed. All of it can't be true. All of it can't be important. But some of it must be.

How do we distinguish between the central and peripheral? Where do we get an orientation in this dizzying whirl of argumentation? How do we find our way home through the blinding storm of controversy? How do we purchase a personal place to stand in the pushing and jostling crowd of people who claim to tell us the truth of our lives?

What gets our attention? The loudest voice? The cleverest slogan? The biggest promise?

On Square Pegs

The present age prepares roles for people and expects us to fit into them. These are roles in which we are asked to smoothly function: as good consumers, as indulgent hedonists, as proud owners, as ruthless competitors, as satisfied customers. But there is a problem: Christians don't fit. People of faith have sharp, awkward edges. We are square pegs in round holes.

Society relentlessly whittles away at those sharp edges so that we will be well adjusted, profitable, and safe. The massive energies of journalism, entertainment, education, and advertising pour over us like the powerful, persistent flowing of water over rock, working to erode us into smooth, secularized surfaces.

We resist. We have been warned by Paul, "Don't let the world around you squeeze you into its own mould, but let God re-mould your minds from within" (Romans 12:2, PHILLIPS). But how do we keep our recovered, original, sharp-edged identity as Christians in a world in which the pressures to conform are so powerful?

Christians have long agreed that our spiritual practices are the core technology for keeping the angles sharp. With prayer and intention, we must encourage and direct the basic practices of faith to maintain our sharp identity—as creatures a little less than God—against the world that is trying constantly to adjust us into the comfortable mediocrity of being little more than animals.

Death, Then Life

A gospel paradox: in getting us ready to live, Jesus gets us ready to die. First he gets himself ready to die so that he can live. Then he gets us ready. Our habit is to think life first, then death. Jesus radicalizes our perceptions: first death, then life. This death is not primarily biological, although it will eventually include that.

Jesus is leading us to the death of illusions, and illusions die hard. Jesus is leading us to the death of self-will, and self-will is a stubborn survivor. Jesus is leading us to the death of sin, and sin is a cat with nine lives. Jesus is leading us to the Lenten death that will catapult us into the Easter resurrection.

Becoming Basic

"He who would do good to another," said poet and painter William Blake, "must do it in Minute Particulars."[*] These days, barraged daily with large headlines that accommodate our imaginations of nations at war, we Christians need to affirm our commitment to the "Minute Particulars" of love and prayer that we can carry out in the immediate circumstances of our lives.

Our opinions and arguments on world affairs make nothing happen, but several times a day, we have chances at peacemaking, praying, and loving that implement the kingdom. Our routines accumulate debris—things we once needed and don't anymore, activities that began as essentials and now produce needless fatigue. We need seasonal house cleanings, otherwise we buy too much and run around too much. Wise Christians get rid of whatever is interfering with who we want to be before God and with each other. Wise Christians go back to the basics.

Take, as one example, the life of Carmelite monk Brother Lawrence, whose words come to us through *The Practice of the Presence of God*. Brother Lawrence was nothing if not basic. He lived with an incredible simplicity and directness. His conversion was characteristic of everything about him. On a midwinter day at the age of eighteen, he saw a dry, leafless tree standing gaunt against the snow. It stirred deep thoughts within

[*] William Blake, "The Holiness of Minute Particulars," *Jerusalem*, 48–53, 60–66, www.bartleby.com/235/322.html.

him of the change the coming spring would bring. At that moment, he decided to be a person in whom the spring would come, letting the life of Christ take root and blossom in his whole being. That's all. It was that simple. The winter tree preached a sermon to him. He repented and believed.

Lawrence became a cook in a monastery and spent *the rest of his life* among pots and pans. He cooked meals, baked bread, and swept the kitchen floor, all the while practicing the presence of God.

For more than three hundred years now, Christians have read his words. They have found peace and fresh energy to return to the basics—to the simple practice of the presence of God. Simple, but not easy. Basic, but not elementary. It takes determined attention to be simple. It takes all the help we can get to be basic.

On Seeds

The Word of God is the seed of the Christian. The Parable of the Sower (see Matthew 13) explains this with unforgettable clarity: the Word comes into our lives with divine power and can, if received rightly, multiply and produce itself in a great harvest to God's glory. The Word of God puts reason, strength, direction, and sense into a Christian's life, and from that point, it is possible for the person to live a new life in Christ, for Christ lives in her. The Word of God is a seed, and as it germinates and grows, the result is the Christian.

But the Christian is the seed of the church. The Christian is to the church what the Word of God is to the Christian—or, analogously, what the seed is to the plant full grown. The church is not just an aggregate of Christians. It is not simply a collective term for talking easily about many individuals who have similar beliefs about God. The church is an entity all its own. It has an organic life with a particular spiritual shape, characteristics, and qualities.

All this is not visible, of course, in either the church or the Christian. Just by looking, it is impossible to tell if someone is a Christian because the life of Christ is a hidden life. It is revealed in many particular visible expressions, true, but its essence is hidden. The same is true with the church. Visibly it looks like a society or institution made up of component parts—individuals who are subscribing to a generally harmonious policy or belief. But from the Word of God, we know something else is really taking place. It is an organic spiritual body, with Christ as head and all of us as members. As we are incorporated into it, we live lives not our own. We become participants in the church's life.

We become seeds.

On Growing Underground

A church is a community for the formation of human beings (made in the image of God) into the stature of Christ. That formation is a complex process, with much of the action invisible and silent. Much of what *is* visible and audible to us is ill formed and unsatisfying. But remember: some seeds stay underground for years before they germinate.

The Good Life

Christians launch daily into lucky* lives—lives of amazing grace, surprised by joy, where they count blessings. They are not easy lives. They are not cozy lives. Christians go to work exploring and experiencing all the details of new life that Christ's birth, death, and resurrection pour into them through the Holy Spirit. They are not explained lives, making neat or perfect sense, but they are *good* lives, robust with a goodness the Christians did not earn. *Lucky.*

---

* Eugene's choice of the word *lucky* has the context of the Greek word *makários* behind it. Eugene was particularly fond of this translation of the word often rendered *blessed* in English, as in the Beatitudes. It does not refer to abstract probability or a divine dice roll. Rather, it carries the everyday power of a child's exclamation at some good fortune: "Lucky!"

Called to Wholeness

From time to time, we fall into the grip of an idea or embrace a behavior that we think is absolutely indispensable for pleasing God and proving our worth to him. Often these ideas and behaviors are completely admirable. The Ten Commandments, for instance—who would find fault with any of us for trying our best to keep them? And who wouldn't admire us if we succeeded?

Jesus finds fault, believe it or not. We get no praise from him at all. In fact, he attacks. He mounts an assault on our moral ideas and our exemplary behavior, which we characteristically construct around us to protect us from having dealings with a personal God—and his love, his mercy, and his purposes of salvation in our lives. One of the most common ways we avoid God is to try to be so good that he will let us alone to be our own gods and run life the way that suits us best. But Jesus won't let us get away with it. He wants us, our hearts, and our warm love-faith relationships with him, not icily correct moral performances before him.

Jesus is famous for the words of comfort that he spoke. Many people yell at us when we get in their way and curse us when we interfere with their plans. The verbal flagellations hurt: we are wounded and degraded; we are humiliated and embarrassed. Words are weapons that can injure and cripple us. The words of Jesus never do that. He is a master at using words in such a way that our very beings are called into wholeness. We listen to him and find ourselves sane and our dignity restored. But while Jesus's words are always hope giving and love deepening, they are not always soothing. Sometimes they are absolutely heartbreaking. Sometimes they are hammer-blows that shatter some fond but wrong idea that we cherish, that demolish some dear idol that we don't think we can live without.

When that happens, it is as if our spiritual hearts contract a disease that interferes with our capacity to vigorously respond to God: our inner muscles lose their elasticity, becoming leathery and hard. Jesus cures us of this condition with heartbreaking words that break up the hardness and restore a supple and easy responsiveness to our souls. He wants something more of us than mere goodness—and his words are meant to call us into love.

The Unspeakable Ordinary

We do not become more spiritual by becoming less material. The life of faith takes place where there are rocks and water. We do not become more Christian by becoming less American or Italian or Norwegian. We do not become more faithful by becoming less a man or woman or youth or child. To grow in Christ, we must not look only for the extraordinary and earth shattering.

The life of faith is mixed with the life of everything else: violence and sex and greed and commerce and government. Realizing the unspeakable ordinariness of the life of faith is powerful.

To Be, to Do

Just to be, just to do—these are the two great gifts of God, the foundations of every other gift. We need to return to these two great capacities again and again and cultivate them.

The events of daily life need to be placed in perspective by a deep sense of prayer, by learning how to be before God. Then, as reality closes in on us, we will perceive each event as the working of the Holy Spirit, carefully designed for our particular needs. Every event is a touch of the living finger of God, which is sketching in us—body, soul, and spirit—the true image of his Son, which the Father originally gave to us and is restoring.

Do You Want to Be Healed?

We are born with an instinctual drive toward excellence. We grow toward wholeness. We reach for the best. We have a thirst for goodness, a hunger for righteousness. And therefore the puzzle is why so many people live so badly. Not so wickedly, but so *inanely*. Not so cruelly, but so *stupidly*.

There is little to admire and less to imitate in most of the people who are prominent in our culture. We have celebrities but not saints. Famous entertainers amuse a nation of bored insomniacs. Infamous criminals act out the aggressions of timid conformists. Petulant and spoiled athletes play games vicariously for lazy and apathetic spectators. People, aimless and bored, amuse themselves with trivia and trash. Neither the adventure of goodness nor the pursuit of righteousness gets headlines.

When we become thoroughly disgusted with the shams that are served up to us daily as celebrities, some of us turn to Scripture to satisfy our need for the best, the excellent. What does it mean to be a real man or a real woman? What shape does mature, authentic humanity take in everyday life?

What we read is apt to surprise us, for we find neither splendid moral examples nor impeccably virtuous models for us to imitate. Abraham lied. Moses murdered and complained. David committed adultery. Peter blasphemed. Jacob cheated. What we find, in fact, is not a perfection but a confrontation. Each person is challenged by God to live a uniquely glorious life of faith in relationship with him.

Jesus addressed a man at the pool of Bethesda: "Do you want to be healed?" (John 5:6, RSV). In that simple question, more is implied: Do you *want* to be whole? Do you *want* to live at your best? I believe the man had become accustomed to living half a life. He had adjusted himself to the average. He had become used to just getting by. He answered Jesus with what might easily be an excuse: "I have no man to put me into the pool" (verse 7, RSV). In other words, "No one will help me." We can hear self-pity in that; perhaps he was even blaming others for his continuing half-life.

It is easy to find reasons to support our present condition. Why did the man not simply say, "Yes, I want to be healed"? Because in some ways it can be easier to be dependent. Not better, but *easier*. Not more meaningful, but *easier*. Not more satisfying, but *easier*.

Jesus bypassed the man's excuse and commanded his wholeness. "Rise, take up your pallet, and walk" (verse 8, RSV). Jesus commands our best and thrusts us into lives of excellence that we never knew we had the strength or capacity to embrace.

A zestful life spills out of the stereotyped containers that our sin-inhibited society provides. We do not have to live another day or another hour "at this poor dying rate."* Jesus knows what we are good for. And with a word, he can make us good at it.

---

* Isaac Watts and John B. Dykes, "Come, Holy Spirit, Heavenly Dove," 1707, public domain, hymnary.org, https://hymnary.org/text/come_holy_spirit_heavenly _dove_with_all.

The Expectant Life

"Expectation . . . is perhaps the supreme Christian function and the most distinctive characteristic of our religion."*

Christians should live on tiptoe. Alert. Joyful. Affirmative. Wide eyed. Ready. What are we looking forward to? In a word, *God*. We know that God comes; it is his most characteristic motion. He doesn't leave. He doesn't wander off. He comes—to us, his people.

In expectation of Christ, we should prepare ourselves to participate wholeheartedly in God's next move. We have a choice to make: Will we live slovenly with unbuttoned mind and disheveled spirit, thoughtlessly supposing that the same things are monotonously repeated over and over in creation and history? Or will we live alertly and ardently, convinced that God still comes and speaks? The expectant command is for us to *awaken*.

Our mission is to develop lives that connect what God did in the past with what he will do in the future. Will we live in spasms and jerks, in fits and starts, in fads and fashions? Or will we live coherently and organically, believing that God will complete what he has begun? The expectant command is for us to *love*.

We ought to cultivate the skills that equip us to live in cheerful anticipation of what God will do tomorrow. Will we

* Pierre Teilhard de Chardin, *The Divine Milieu* (New York: Perennial, 2001), 130.

live anxiously, complaining and querulous, because we don't have all we want or because we don't know what is coming next? Or will we live in confident joy, sure that God's next move will be a good one? The expectant command is for us to *rejoice*.

Shaping Belief

The act of belief is the single most significant thing about us. Our beliefs are far more important than our bank accounts, our reputations, or our schooling. Successful crooks have large bank accounts, undetected hypocrites have glowing reputations, and highly educated people pursue evil ends.

Belief shapes character, results in behavior, and gives coherence to life. An animal can be described in terms of behavior and habitat, but only belief will account for a human being. If we are concerned only with saving our own skin, have no awareness of God, or take no responsibility regarding ancestors and descendants, we cannot be said to truly *live* as human beings at all.

But the word *belief* is in poor repute. It has become tepid and murky, a dishwater word. James, dismayed by what happened to the worldly belief among Christians in the first century, wrote in anger and dismay, "You believe that God is one; you do well. Even the demons believe—and shudder" (2:19). People in the community to which James wrote made proud assertions of belief in God but simultaneously treated the person that God created with cruelty and contempt. In a single generation, they had brought a noble, robust word into disrepute. *Belief,* for them, was a religious emotion—a mere fluttering of the soul in the presence of the sublime.

But the emotion left no more impression on their lives than a footstep in the sand. The next wave of emotion (of anger this time, of enthusiasm the next) wiped out all traces. Devils have emotions like that! *Belief* used as a synonym for *emotion* is meaningless—a dead word. True belief requires resurrection, the resurrection that comes through personal commitment to Jesus Christ as Lord and Savior.

Belief that doesn't involve personal commitment to God is meaningless—a frivolous emotion. Belief should be the all-involving act of our lives. What it involves us in is what God is doing. The center of the action is God: he is creating, and he is saving; he is blessing, and he is preserving. The world is electric with meaning, fascinating in its beauty, alive with action—because the God of creation is in action. Belief involves us in participation in God's action in the world.

It is a great waste and blasphemy when people are glib in the language of belief but avoid the everyday action of God.

On Living It Up

Has life gone flat on you? Is the old zest gone? Has life become, as James Michener suggested, "a falling-away, a gradual surrender of the dream"?* It has for many. Morals get flabby. Goals lose their magnetism. Imagination goes slack.

But no one was created to live listlessly. No one is fated to boredom. God did not design this marvelous creation and invest us with eternal hungers and thirsts with the expectation that we would sit around and in fatigued voices ask, "What's next?"

"Living the good life," philosopher Nikolai Berdyaev is said to have written, "is frequently dull and flat and commonplace."† Our greatest problem, he claimed, is to make it fiery and creative and capable of spiritual struggle.

Jesus, in his parables and example, wakes us up to the central vitalities of life, the realities that provoke intensity and participation and commitment. His example prompts us to live upward toward God, to live on tiptoe, to live in such a way that our lives increase and develop with the energies of God's grace. Christ's way of life is a holy attack on everything that leaks the brightness out of our lives or detracts from the promised joy of our faith. It demolishes anything that promises liberation but, in fact, imprisons us in boredom. Following him evokes a life pursued heartily and meaningfully.

---

* James A. Michener, *Sports in America* (New York: Random House, 2015), 286.
† Nikolai Berdyaev, quoted in Andrew Sheehan, ed., *The Essential Sheehan: A Lifetime of Running Wisdom from the Legendary Dr. George Sheehan* (New York: Rodale, 2013), 18.

On Dreams and Visions

M ost of life consists of what we cannot usually see. Dreams and visions are means of seeing the reality that is inaccessible to our senses. We use microscopes to see the very small, we use telescopes to see the very far away, and we use dreams and visions to see the truth. There are strong forces around us that externalize us—that diminish the rich interiors of our lives and reduce us to what we can see and pick up and buy. That is the world's work. That is sin's work. We define ourselves by what we can put on a job description. God gives us dreams and visions so that we have access to the whole thing: the world for which Christ died, the whole person in whom Christ lives.

Think of some of the stories in the Bible: Abraham's vision, Jacob's dream, Balaam's vision, Solomon's dream, Mary's vision, and Joseph's dream. Every time we read of one of these dreams or visions, a life deepens and the world changes. Do you expect it would be different for us? Visions are essential in life.

Leap, Live, Love

God invites us to leap, to live, and to love: to *leap* from the visible uncertainties of self to the invisible certainties of faith, to *live* intensely instead of eagerly and dully, and to *love* directly and personally and not secondhand.

Each person, says the gospel, is called to leap in faith, to live as his or her own authentic and personal being, and to love, perhaps for the first time, intimately. Christ shows us in his own life how to do this in a way that does not require us to curb our own uniqueness, joy, or excellence. Rather, it is expanded.

On Shouting for Crumbs

Just then a Canaanite woman from that region came out and started shouting, "Have mercy on me, Lord, Son of David; my daughter is tormented by a demon." But he did not answer her at all. And his disciples came and urged him, saying, "Send her away, for she keeps shouting after us."

Matthew 15:22–23

The woman had chutzpah, and that catches our attention. She badgered Jesus to the point of irritation and nagged him into compassion. Saint Matthew told her story in his gospel and opened a dimension of experience that we often suppress.

Maybe we don't have to compose ourselves into postures of reverence before we pray. Maybe we don't have to know very much about the strategies of salvation before we appeal for help. Maybe when we feel excluded from the rich banquet of life that everyone else seems to have such easy access to, we need to push our way into the room—elbow our way to the head table and demand at least a portion of the leftovers.

This is not the polite approach to Jesus that we are taught by our pastors and parents, but it worked once.

Maybe it will work again.

A Lavish God

Take what belongs to you and go; I choose to give to this last the same as I give to you. Am I not allowed to do what I choose with what belongs to me? Or are you envious because I am generous?

Matthew 20:14–15

A generous God is hard to get used to.

In the course of growing up and finding our way in the world, we accumulate a lot of guilt. We assume that God—if there is a God—is just waiting for the right time to let us have it, to punish us and put us in our place.

And then Jesus tells us the surprising opposite.

The Struggle Makes Sense

The Christian life is an invitation to hear something good—not something sad, morose, or tragic. One of the fruits of the Christian life is joy. Praise and gladness are characteristic marks of the worship that Christians offer.

What we have, you see, is a style of joy, a quality of gladness that achieves its inner quality not by avoiding sin or by side-stepping evil or by carefully constructing one's life so that one will not be troubled by misfortune. What we have is a joy so powerful, a gladness so ultimate, that it can confront what is tragic and overcome it. Christian good news is solid enough that it can absorb the world's bad news and still maintain itself as good news.

One recalls a short fable: Two frogs fell into a jar half full of cream. One frog soberly appraised the situation, realized struggle was useless, put its little fingers together, and drowned. The other frog was not so intellectual and did not stop to analyze the situation. Since it did not have the same information as the other frog, it went on struggling for its life. The rapid strokes of the frog's hands gradually thickened the cream and created a lump of butter. The emotional frog crawled onto this solid lump and jumped out of the jar.

That's not a bad summary of the Christian faith: a declaration that the struggle makes sense. I'm no better at explanations of what's wrong with the world than anybody else. But I can bear witness that people can experience the deepest kind of humiliation and rejection and still have life make sense, finally, because God worked in them. I can bear witness that the suffering that Jesus experienced and confronted didn't produce a morose, depressed man but rather resulted in the gospel, the good news. And I can bear witness that when I share the sufferings of others and confront the despair of life, I find another power working in me—the grace of Jesus Christ—that puts things together again in a way that feels strangely like joy.

PART TWO

On Simplicity

I'm not saying that I have this all together, that I have it made. But I am well on my way, reaching out for Christ, who has so wondrously reached out for me. Friends, don't get me wrong: By no means do I count myself an expert in all of this, but I've got my eye on the goal, where God is beckoning us onward—to Jesus. I'm off and running, and I'm not turning back.

Philippians 3:12–14, MSG

A Welcoming

G od comes to us. (He doesn't go away.)
God arrives in our world. (He doesn't depart into outer space.)

God enters our condition. (He doesn't hold himself aloof from the mess we are in.)

But an arrival is not complete until there is a welcoming; a visit is not satisfying if there is no greeting. Are we ready to welcome God? Are we alert to greet him? Are we practicing the skills of hospitality with which we receive him and make him welcome in our lives and world?

On the Overlook

Some things we overlook because they are so small. Others we overlook because they are so large, such as when people who live at the base of a huge mountain never look at it anymore, although they did often enough when they were children. But the mountain is the most significant geographical feature in their lives, shaping the weather, determining the soil, marking boundaries.

God is huge in that way—obvious, essential, inescapable—but even more so, for he is also personal and passionate and gracious and merciful. His outer largeness ("the heavens are telling the glory of God" [Psalm 19:1]) is matched by an inner largeness ("the joy of your salvation" [51:12]). We've all seen it, exclaimed over it, and been changed by it. But year after year of living in a world of such magnitude makes it easy to quit seeing it and to lose awareness of God in the urgent and everyday business of getting across the street without getting hit by an 18-wheeler. That is why we work together as a community to have awareness of the great presence of God in our lives. We seek to wake ourselves up, to make sure that the roar of the vacuum cleaner doesn't drown out the knock of the treasured Guest at the door, to deliberately step out of the fast lane so that we can see and hear and touch the God who is around and within us and can shut up long enough so that we hear and truly listen to the story of God coming to us, born in Jesus. Born in us.

On Being Biblical

We do not qualify as biblical simply by quoting the Bible. We are biblical only when we share life in the wilderness with those who are tempted and fall, when we carry the cross of Jesus, and when we love extravagantly in Jesus's name.

On Doing Less

Many of us seem to have picked up our ideas of what being a good Christian is from experiences we've accumulated in our early years of growing up. Some of us learned then that being good daughters or sons, being good boys or girls, meant helping out in some way or other: picking up the trash, doing the dishes, making our beds, or sharing our toys. We began life being taken care of totally, then gradually learned to take care of ourselves, relieving our parents of those duties, and then went on to take care of others.

But being Christians is nearly the opposite of that. Being Christians means letting God take care of us, totally. We usually begin by trying to find out what we can do to help, expecting as we go along that we will take on more and more responsibility, getting busier and busier in the Lord's service. What we find, though, is that as we become practiced in the practices of prayer and worship and trust and love, we are more and more *receivers* and our lives are experienced as gifts, as grace.

There is a paradox here: the less busy we are, the more free we are to do the essentially Christian acts. The less we hassle ourselves and one another with jobs, lists, and endless moralistic housecleaning, the more focused we become for truly productive lives of creation and vocation.

The less we do, the more we find our Lord the Spirit doing in and through us.

The Jesus Risk

Jesus is not a sure thing. We risk our very lives when we follow him. We want God on our side so that we will have security, but Jesus calls us to a life full of hazard. We enter into the act of worship and expose our lives to Scripture and find something far better than a sure thing. We find a living Lord and an active faith full of unpredictability. William Stafford's poem "A Course in Creative Writing" contrasts what we cautiously want with what we get when we live in faith:

> They want a wilderness with a map—
> but how about errors that give a new start?*

Jesus's story is our training ground for living at risk, living expectantly, and living with a Lover who daily surprises us with grace.

---

* William Stafford, *You Must Revise Your Life* (Ann Arbor: University of Michigan, 1986), 52.

Faith Is Not a Lobotomy

The Christian faith does not turn us into robots who are conditioned to behave in moral ways by reflex. The Christian faith does not lobotomize us so that we don't have to think through anything. Jesus said, "Learn from me" (Matthew 11:29). He intends to shape our minds, inform our intelligence, and mature our judgment so that we can understand and participate in the meaning of new life.

Possible Impossibilities

There is a dizzying, disorienting quality to Jesus's words, as recorded in his teaching and parables. *What is he talking about anyway?* we think. *Is this airhead preaching? Isn't religion supposed to make us well-adjusted citizens? Doesn't God want us to live moderately and serenely?* But every time we return to the gospel records and read again exactly what is there, we realize afresh how much of what Jesus said doesn't fit at all into what we think of as a normal life. And we realize how habitually we reduce his words to what fits into what we call the "real world." Our so-called real world is real enough, but it is a much-reduced world, a gray world, a flat-earth world.

Jesus's words bring us the news of an expanded world, a bright world, a full-dimensioned world—a world in which God rules, mercy is a common experience, and love is the daily working agenda, not an occasional romantic interlude. Jesus's words orient us to the world that is changed from the inside out by his arrival and rule.

Ordinary Secrets

The most extraordinary feature of the gospel is its ordinariness. The fact that the Word that created the heavens and arranges the seasons enters *ordinary* lives and fashions eternal life in them is truly extraordinary.

And isn't it extraordinary that these ordinary lives that are radically transformed by grace continue to appear so ordinary? A man who has spent fifty-two years making a mess of his life encounters the living God in Jesus Christ, believes and obeys, and becomes an absolutely new creature. Everything is changed from the inside out, from top to bottom. But when he gets out of bed the next day and walks out into the street, he is still five feet seven, weighs 164 pounds, and has age spots on the backs of his hands and a cut on his jaw from too-hasty shaving, and when he talks, he pronounces his words in a way that indicates he was born and raised in Texas. To everyone who sees and listens to him, he looks and sounds the same. *Is someone keeping a secret?*

A woman who has lived selfishly and indulgently for thirty-two years encounters the living God in Jesus Christ, believes and obeys, and becomes an absolutely new creature. She begins to love extravagantly—to forgive and to serve. But when she looks in the mirror the next day, she still sees one chin more than she would prefer, the onset of crow's-feet at the edges of her eyes, and gray hairs that she has been distressed at seeing recently. When she walks into the kitchen, she moves with the same slightly pigeon-toed gait that her friends have kidded her about for most of her life. *What is all this about being a "new creature"?* she wonders. *Is there some secret ingredient?*

One of the extraordinary things about Jesus was that he unassumingly took his place among the ordinary men and women around him. Even after his resurrection, he appeared *ordinary.* Mary at the tomb looked at him and thought he was the gardener (see John 20:15). Two disciples on the Emmaus road thought he was just another traveler (see Luke 24:28–29). The disciples fishing on the Sea of Galilee didn't recognize him on the shore (see John 21:1–4). Hundreds of people saw him walking along the roads and heard him talking to his friends and family and had no idea that God was in him, among them.

Why the secrecy? He didn't make it easy for us to see God in him. But there were occasional and brief moments when the glory broke through blazingly and recognition was immediate. The Baptism was one of these moments; the Transfiguration, another.

These moments, despite the ordinary secrecy, continue to occur.

A Sudden Longing

Jacob's well was there, and Jesus, tired out by his journey, was sitting by the well. It was about noon.

A Samaritan woman came to draw water, and Jesus said to her, "Give me a drink."

John 4:6–7

She was surprised out of her socks, really. She was on her way to get a bucket of water, a job she had done a couple of times every day for who-knows-how-many years. A stranger started a conversation with her, which also happened frequently. She was attractive enough. Five times in her life, conversations like this had ended up in marriage. She responded with teasing banter, a conversational style natural to her.

Within minutes, the conversation opened up hungers and thirsts she had forgotten she ever had. These went beyond anything that could be satisfied by a drink from a bucket of water or going to bed with a man. She realized her desperate need for God, her long-suppressed passion for him.

It might have made sense if she had been a religious person or been on her way to church. But she was anything but religious, and she was a long way from church. Now here she was, on a Tuesday noon, pulling a bucket of water out of a well and discovering God in her life.

This kind of thing happens all the time. And it happens to

all of us. We meet God when we least expect it in places that we never would have guessed. In the middle of routines, a sudden longing is released and comes out into the open. While passing the time of day, we hear God's Word spoken and life is changed.

Jesus did—and does—this a lot. He finds us as we are, going about our work and thinking that God is a million miles away, and engages us in conversations that change our lives. There is no style of life that exempts us from these meetings, there is no day of the week on which it may not happen, and there is no work that may not provide the scene for an encounter.

Down-to-Earth Religion

Religion that is pure and undefiled before God, the Father, is this: to care for orphans and widows in their distress, and to keep oneself unstained by the world.

James 1:27

I was visiting with several friends once. We were talking about how we had entered the faith and found ourselves in relation with Jesus Christ. One of my friends, in the course of affirming how personal Jesus was to him, quite vehemently protested, "But I am not religious." He repeated the denial a couple of times to make sure we got it.

We got it.

Religious is a negative word for a lot of people. I think I understand why. For many, *religious* means fussing around with words and manners and petty, half-important projects. It means a safe and harmless thing that I once heard called "kitchen religion" and has nothing to do with the words that came crashing down from Sinai or the blood that poured off Golgotha.

It is an old problem, this trivialization of God and the gospel, and needs to be faced and fought continuously. In the first-generation church, the fight was led by James. He wrote a letter, circulated through the first-century congregation, in which he said, like my friend the other evening, "I am not religious" (paraphrasing, see James 1:26). He took the word *religion* (which was getting a bad reputation in the world), shook it out, scrubbed it up, and restored it to its glorious and exhilarating original.

We must return to the basics of life together in Christ. We must clear the ground and make sure we are starting our journeys on the right foot. We must rediscover a better "religion."

On Religion and Faith

"When the Son of Man comes, will he find faith on earth?" (Luke 18:8). Surely he will find *religion* (institutions, creeds, documents, artifacts, and the like), but he may not find *faith*. Faith is deeply personal, dynamic, and ultimate. Religion, however, is faith's expression. For example, religion is concerned about institutions (churches), documents, statements of belief (Bible and theology), and our convictions and moral codes. Religion is important but not ultimately important.

Religion is a means, not an end. Faith is the only end.

The Inside Story

We need exercise in getting our feet on the ground and making sure we are headed in the right direction. The "ground" of our lives is holy ground; the "right direction" is toward the Cross of Jesus. Clutter drifts into our lives, obscuring the holy ground. Voices call out conflicting counsel. We must simplify the clutter and listen to the single voice.

We must choose to cultivate our inwardness. Spiritual practices, including prayer and fasting, are about getting our inside stories straight. Most of the life of Jesus took place behind the scenes, in prayer. Everything that we know of Jesus—his words and his acts—is a revelation of a vast "working out" of salvation at the heart of the world. It is not enough to become knowledgeable in surface facts. It is not enough to gain access to the biblical reports. We need the inside story, the God-story, that is at the heart of everything.

Prayer grants access to inwardness, to the God-action that is taking place within us. This God-action is the most distinctive thing about us. It is more important than our circulatory systems, our brain waves, and our skeletal structures. When we realize that huge centrality, we are no longer content with prayers that are brief and occasional expressions of thanks or general laments upward. We want something comprehensive—prayer that is rigorously probing and capable of getting at the entire inside stories of our lives.

A Packaged God Is No God at All

If the word *God* or the experience of God is tribalized or nationalized or privatized, it is falsified. A packaged god is no god at all. This fact is not always easy to live with.

Our tendency, most of the time, is to reduce God to the dimensions of our lives and make him the custodian of our comforts. We get a piece of the gospel that makes us feel good, and we decide to specialize in that part, leaving out everything else. We come across a few friends we like worshipping with and find ourselves guarding the coziness and excluding others.

And then we open our Bibles and read these early experiences of God and the church and realize that we can't disregard others—not if we want to be a real church. We have to reach out, letting our lives be stretched with new challenges, new people, and new experiences.

The Deeper Need

> As for me, my feet had almost stumbled;
> my steps had nearly slipped.
> For I was envious of the arrogant;
> I saw the prosperity of the wicked.
>
> Psalm 73:2–3

I don't yet have what I want. My life is a kind of need factory that runs twenty-four hours a day, seven days a week. The need for food that was satisfied with a bowl of oatmeal at breakfast is back again at noon demanding soup and a sandwich. The need for clothing that not only warms but also enhances and expresses who I am requires periodic fashionable updating to meet my insatiable need for social approval.

People around me, finding out that I have these needs, find ways to exploit them. They do it to make money. Quite clearly, they stimulate my sense of need and then channel it into ways that they promise to meet for a price. The need they start with is usually legitimate, but then it is distorted and twisted into rampant and out-of-control greed.

A waiting heart deliberately interrupts this process in which our needs become corrupted by covetousness. We are returned to our basic needs, our God-need, and are directed to take care of *that*. Fundamentally, we take care of it by praying.

With God as the first item on our lists of needs, we are directed to prayer, where we deal with God personally (truly, the only way he can be dealt with).

We *pray*. And as we pray out our God-need, we find to our surprise that it doesn't go away. The need remains. It not only remains but also deepens. And so we find ourselves waiting— for wholeness, for the coming of Christ. Waiting can make us impatient and irritable, or it can make us more and more helpful and ready. Waiting, for the praying Christian, is a gospel art.

Ordinary Care

Caring for others is the best thing we do. We are at our best when we are attending to the needs of others: hurts and pains, sorrows and disappointments, despair and grief, confusion and dismay. Speaking words of encouragement, binding up wounds, giving direction, sharing trouble—when we are doing these things, we are being fully human. We never feel shamed or guilty or mean when we do such things. We don't always do them well, and sometimes we do them badly.

Caring for others requires skill and stamina, intelligence and discipline. It is not something we can do occasionally when we feel a gush of sentiment. Life together as people of God is, among other things, training in caring for others. We cannot be fully human if we do not do this. We cannot enjoy and delight in the gospel if we do not do this. And so we refuse to quit caring when our caring is flawed. We refuse to pass the buck for caring to others. We commit ourselves to a lifelong apprenticeship in the practice of caring for others.

The letter to the Hebrews includes a succinct text to keep us attentive to this feature of life together: "Let mutual love continue. Do not neglect to show hospitality to strangers, for by doing that some have entertained angels without knowing it" (13:1–2). The text brings to mind a story: Abraham at the oaks of Mamre (see Genesis 18:1–8).

Abraham towers in our regard as the one for whom God was everything. He lived in a vast, soaring, splendid world of grace. He believed. That is why he is important to us. He is evidence that we are totally alive only when we live by faith in God. But there is a less publicized side to Abraham: he cared for others skillfully. A passionate concern for God didn't render him indifferent to people. One day three men showed up at his tent, and Abraham greeted them and invited them to stay for a meal. He did not treat them as interruptions to his prayers or as intrusions on his pilgrimage.

The spontaneity of Abraham's hospitality shows that it was part and parcel of his faith. It seems he treated everyone that way. He didn't know that the men were angels. According to C. S. Lewis, "There are no *ordinary* people. . . . Next to the Blessed Sacrament itself, your neighbour is the holiest object presented to your senses."*

Caring begins in the ordinary. Caring doesn't mean dramatic intervention. Rather, it develops out of the routine courtesies: meals shared, greetings exchanged, silences accented, and affirmations ventured. We don't all do the same things. We don't all have the same gifts. Skillful caring is fashioned out of the natural circumstances of life with whoever happens to be there. We don't have to be in extraordinary happenings with conspicuous gifts faced with overwhelming needs.

Abraham in front of his tent. A hastily prepared meal. Angels unawares.

* C. S. Lewis, *The Weight of Glory: And Other Addresses* (New York: Harper-Collins, 2001), 46.

What Do We Do?

Once I had a conversation with a new acquaintance. He was engaged in work with which I was unfamiliar, so I asked him what he did. He told me in rapid-fire sentences for about twenty minutes.

Reflecting on the meeting afterward, I realized that I *still* didn't know what he did—what he really *did*. I knew the number of meetings he set up, the large numbers of people he spoke to, and the impressive mileage that he logged in travel. But his language had been mostly cliché, so it was nearly impossible to pick up anything specific or distinctively personal.

I ended up knowing a lot about his activities but very little about him—about that conjunction of inner and outer that takes place in real work, that distillation of purpose and passion that gets expressed in this Christian way. I had anticipated a conversation with a potential friend; what I got was a presentation by a religious salesperson. I was disappointed.

Then a friend told me a contrasting story. The same question was put to a person busily at work: "What are you doing?" But instead of a job description or a list of tasks and accomplishments, the quiet answer was this: "I'm changing the world." That is a Saint Paul kind of answer: *I'm changing the world*. It is also a church kind of answer: *We're changing the world*. I don't know if you have something quite that large in mind when you prepare to come to worship. Maybe you just expect a little inspiration or solace. Maybe you just want to get away for an hour or two from life's daily clutter and be refreshed by some beauty and sacred order. Maybe you are following an old habit. But we are changing the world.

Every time the Word of God is proclaimed, creation is in motion again. Every time the Holy Spirit is invoked, salvation is in motion again. Every time we open our mouths in praise, confess our faith with our lips, and believe in our hearts, the world changes.

The Roots of the World

The spoken and written word is active; it does things, makes things happen. It is so easy to lose connection with this reality and let ourselves be intimidated by force and might, by horsepower and nuclear power, by money and militancy, and by terrorism and brutality. But there are times when even the newspapers report this truth: the real action in the world is rooted in words.

Václav Havel* sat in prison in Czechoslovakia for many years because the communist government was afraid of his words and what his words would do. Havel had little interest in politics and did not write about politics—he was a deeply committed Christian who wrote plays for the stage and letters to his wife. Why would anyone consider him dangerous? Only because he wrote truth, wrote well, and used words that were full of energy.

But even though they imprisoned him, they couldn't keep his words in the cell. And then, nine months after we watched with astonishment the collapse of communism in Eastern Europe, he stepped out of prison and was immediately made president of his country. In the speeches he made after that remarkable reversal, he spoke over and over again to the Word, to the nature of the Word, to the Word of God and the Word made flesh.

But not all words are active. Separated from the life of God,

* "Václav Havel: President of Czech Republic," *Britannica,* www.britannica.com
  /biography/Vaclav-Havel.

the Spirit of God, words are paltry. Words used without accuracy, without passion, and without love are lifeless. It is not enough to open our mouths and guess. It is not enough to make more or less articulate sounds come out of our mouths. Words that make and root the world, that bring truth into lives, and that ignite love in hearts are the words that are born in the presence of God.

And that is why the church ordains men and women to this ministry of the Word. The single-minded task of these ministers of the Word is to maintain the living connection—to be steeped in the silence of prayer so that the Word of God can be heard and answered, new every morning, fresh again and again.

On Work

Work. The Christian faith is physical. It takes place, every bit of it, in materiality: caulking a cracked sidewalk, washing windows, trimming azaleas, pointing eroded masonry, fixing a broken pipe, and hauling debris to the landfill. It also includes healing a hurt body, training the brain to recognize truth, and disciplining bodies to behave in acts of justice and love.

Prayer. The Christian faith is spiritual. It takes place, every bit of it, in acts of faith that are invisible: believing in the real presence of the Christ we do not see, loving people around us when they don't seem to deserve it and we don't feel like it, and expecting the arrival of the kingdom of God at the very moment journalists are announcing the latest sleaze.

Everything physical is at the same time spiritual. Everything spiritual is at the same time physical. There is no separating these realities. The Saturday workers and the Sunday worshippers are the same people. Everything we do, on both days, can be to the glory of God—or *could have been* for his glory, for the physicality and spiritualty of both work and prayer can be perverted into prideful sin.

Necessary Words

Words are never truly empty. Words—real words, *true words*—get under our skin and shape our lives. Words make us from the inside out. When the Word is preached or taught, said or sung, prayed or meditated, that is not the end of it. God continues to watch over this Word, tending it and caring for it until it brings forth love, obedience, hope, belief, or joy. And we watch with him—not as spectators at a ball game but as shepherds of a flock, as parents of a child, as lovers and friends—watching for signs of grace, watching for movements of joy, watching for evidence that once again the Word has become flesh. Watching over the Word is neither obvious nor easy. But it is necessary.

And because it is not obvious or easy but is necessary, the church ordains ministers of the Word to also be ministers of the sacrament—to spot the connections, to doggedly stay with the people to whom the Word has been proclaimed, praying persistently and vigilantly with them and for them, to alertly watch over this Word of God until it becomes the performance of God.

It is so easy to miss this part. It is so easy to proclaim this Word and then walk off and do something else, to get distracted, to get busy. But God has promised that he is going to watch over this Word to perform it. We need to stick around and see what happens, and pastors need to lead their congregations to stick around and see what happens, to see how God performs this Word. Congregations are great wanderers: ten minutes after having heard the Word of God, they lose interest and turn on the television or go shopping or eat a snack. And then they are not around to witness the performance of the Word.

Pastors are great wanderers too. After having preached and taught the Word, they abandon the people in whom God has promised to perform the Word and are not around to witness the performance in their lives. Everything that goes on in people's lives is, or can be, connected with the Word that is proclaimed. God is watching over the Word to perform it. And we watch with him because we don't want to miss out on a thing that comes out of these words that God puts in our mouths.

How Much Reality?

> In the morning, while it was still very dark, he got up and went out to a deserted place, and there he prayed. And Simon and his companions hunted for him. When they found him, they said to him, "Everyone is searching for you."
>
> Mark 1:35–37

D oes being with Jesus reduce or enlarge our lives? Does Jesus contain us in a small world of cozy domesticity or lead us into a large world of demanding exploration? It is alarming when we observe how meagerly so many people live; our alarm increases when these meager lives are labeled "Christian."

Is this what the search for Christ results in? Caution? Playing it safe? Predictable approval? How much reality are we prepared for when following Jesus? A lot or a little? We can, it seems, get by on minimal reality, supplementing it with large doses of fantasy and labeling the supplements "Christian." But our alarm decreases when we examine the gospel stories carefully.

Jesus is always leading us into more. We can enter the real world.

Launched to Holiness

With joy you will draw water from the wells of salvation.

Isaiah 12:3

I frequently hear pastors and others lament that people don't go to church the way they used to. Worshipping God is no longer a priority in people's lives. Sunday morning is self-indulgence time, a time to take it easy, and a chance to treat number one to some quality time. And what a lot of options there are! Strolls, entertainment, visits to zoos and museums, sunning on the beach, fishing, smelling the flowers—is it any wonder that worship no longer takes top billing on Sunday mornings?

But my voice will not be heard among the laments. I am astonished that anybody worships at all. What are all these people doing in church each Sunday? Why on earth be here when they have all these attractive and promising options? Going to church on a Sunday morning made sense when everybody in the village did it—when the pressure of tradition and the custom of centuries dictated it and the pastor exercised powerful moral authority over the entire community. (Besides, what else was there to do on a Sunday morning?) But now people have options: well-advertised, socially sanctioned options, any one of which promises more zip than an hour of worship. In the face of the formidable competition, why do all these people, millions of them every week, keep showing up to worship God? I am far more astonished that people do come than distressed that they don't.

Why do they do it? Why do *we* do it? It is simple.

We come to *see*—to get our vision cleared of the ugliness and trash so that we can see what God is doing at the heart of it.

We come to *hear*—to clear our ears of the noise of anger and lust that pollute the atmosphere and to listen to love spoken to our hearts, forgiveness to our sins, mercy to our failures, and grace to our needs.

We come to *touch*—to break through the social makeup and protective role-playing and touch one another in greetings of welcome and acceptance.

And we come to *speak*—not words that flatter or sell or manipulate but ones that speak what we most deeply are and feel, that honestly confess our sin, and that reverently sing our praise. Lives turn around, open up, and come alive in the act of worship.

For evidence of this life, look at Isaiah. Isaiah was one of the most wide-awake, in-touch, well-spoken people ever. It all started for him in an act of worship. He knew what was going on around him—in the city, in politics, and in people. He also knew what was going on inside him and inside the events of the day. He knew what God was doing: he saw the holiness, he heard the commands, he felt the cleansing, and he spoke his commitment to the faith.

The facts reported in the newspapers and described in our textbooks are real enough, but they are the miniscule edge of reality. There is far, far more. Worship launches us into the rich, invisible inflow of holiness—the action and Word of God.

Three Short Thoughts on Direction

All life is a pilgrimage. We are on our way to a destination. Christians believe that we are on our way to God and that our companion is Jesus Christ.

One of the primary (maybe *the* primary) signposts showing the way is the Cross of Jesus.

On Thinking and Thanking

Have you ever noticed the close relationship between the words *think* and *thank*? The change of a single vowel triggers a quantum leap in meaning.

Thinking is a work of the mere intellect; thanking is an expression of the whole person. Thanking that is not preceded by thinking is shallow and inadequate, but thinking that does not transform to thanking is arid and sterile.

It is our acts of gratitude that complete our processes of worship and remembrance. We recollect all that has happened among us by Christ's design. We praise the Lord, who makes our lives, like all things, work together for good. Is there any other place in our society where so much is remembered and praised as here among Christians in worship, where there is such a concentration of memory and such exuberance in gratitude? I *think* not.

Changes

M ost of us don't like change. It usually means work on our part and adjustments and variations to our normal way of doing things. Sometimes, though, we long for change to occur. Life isn't quite what we had hoped for, and we look for something new.

In both cases, those times of transition are usually a bit difficult and most always involve some work on our part. It is how we approach that work and how we see God involved in the changes that make all the difference. God is shaping. His hand is molding. We can discover his ways in the changes of our own lives.

Change will probably always be uncomfortable. But we can begin to see it as desirable because the One who knows us best is carefully orchestrating the transitions of our lives.

Wisdom? Wealth?

Neither wisdom nor wealth can save us. Neither PhDs nor fat salaries can bring us to God as free men and women. Neither education nor prosperity can guarantee the good life. Our thinking power and our earning power combined are not enough to usher in utopia.

This in no way detracts from the usefulness or desirability of intelligence and wealth. Education is certainly one of the major liberating factors in our civilization, and prosperity is a major benefit. In Solomon's life, his wisdom and wealth were admired rather than despised. But they were not capable of freeing him from his sins and bringing the rule of God to the people. There was a central omission, and because of that defect, nothing worked out. Then his wisdom turned to folly and his wealth to decadence. With all his gifts, Solomon failed to do what the shorter catechism says we must do: "glorify God, and . . . enjoy him forever."*

We have particular reason for noting Solomon's life, for we today are facing similar possibilities. Because of the culture we live in, each one of us has a good chance of being both wealthy and wise. We know a lot and we have a lot. Yet there are many indications that we are not using our wisdom and wealth according to God's will.

There are large pockets of poverty in our land. The world has millions of hungry people. Surely it is not the will of God

---

* Westminster Shorter Catechism, answer to question 1, public domain; see "Shorter Catechism," the Orthodox Presbyterian Church, www.opc.org/sc.html.

that people be hopelessly trapped in desperate poverty at a time when our culture as a whole has become one of affluence and abundance. Beyond economics, beyond politics, this is an issue of love (or the deplorable lack of it).

We must look for a deeper reason for living than simply acquiring better educations and better jobs and more wisdom and more wealth. We must seek a more substantial means of glorifying God—deeper wisdom and a greater amount of wealth than Solomon's. We must take steps to protect ourselves from Solomon's paradox: the outward signs of wisdom and wealth that cover up an inward stupidity and a social poverty.

That means that we will have to begin not on the outside but on the inside, not with the superstructure but with the foundation. We begin with ourselves as creatures of God and seek his wisdom and wealth at our deepest levels of being. We seek them through Jesus Christ.

Saint John spoke of our Lord as the "Word" of God—that is, the intelligence or the rationality of God. He also called him the "glory" of God. The word *glory* in Hebrew (*kabod*) means much the same as wealth—solid wealth. We speak of receiving Christ into our hearts, receiving God's kindness and nearness within our own existence. When we do this voluntarily, the Word of God and the glory of God, his truth and his grace, his wisdom and his wealth, become implanted as life principles within us. Our lives begin to reflect the rationality of divinity and the solid wealth of eternity.

It still may not be judged as either wisdom or wealth by this world (our Lord died poor and reckoned by Pilate as a fool), but we will be wise in the counsel of God and inheritors of the riches of a new heaven and new earth.

We Are Not Exempt

I don't want any one of us to be naive about what is involved in living this Christian life in community. The proclaimed Word of God brings us into response to God's love, his saving will being worked out in our lives. That is the most wonderful, life-deepening, soul-transforming thing that happens.

But other things also happen: dark forces within us protest; people around us don't like it. When that happens, I don't want you to be disheartened. I don't want you to quit. I don't want you to conclude that you are doing this all wrong and that if you were just a better person, things would go better for you.

Perhaps in your Christian community right now there is commitment and enthusiasm, willingness and cheerfulness. Perhaps the community is welcoming and serving. Nobody throws rocks at the pastor in the pulpit. Crowds don't gather outside and shout curses at you as you drive out of the parking lot. Ugly graffiti is not spray-painted on the buildings. But it won't always be that way. We are not exempt from hard times. Every page of Scripture documents the opposition that develops when the life of Christ is lived sacrificially and honestly.

While we should celebrate good news, we must not be naive about evil. If we do this right, we are going to be as cheerful and faithful in the hard times as we are in the good times—cheerful and faithful like Paul and Barnabas, refusing to let anything difficult or discouraging deter us from living for the glory of God.

This Is the Boldness

P salms are the most accurate mirrors of the human heart we have. It is significant that they say these two things: humanity is involved deeply in unhappiness and wrongdoing, and God is cosmically involved in both a glorious creation and a gracious redemption.

As Christians, this is the boldness in which we should participate. We must be bold in admitting who we are: people who fall far short of God's will and who often are active accomplices in plans to thwart or destroy his will. If at any time we fail to do this, we become self-righteous, arrogant, pontifical, and almost insufferable to those outside the church.

Early in the service of worship, many Christians say a prayer of confession—not to condemn or make themselves feel low and worthless but to get the whole human affair into perspective and have a base from which to work. This confession is important. But we must be equally bold in proclaiming God's mighty acts: "God raised him up" (Acts 2:24). It is for this we exist: to tell a world already full of doubt, skepticism, contradictory evidence, hopelessness, sorrow, and death that God is the creator and redeemer, that God loves his creatures and will redeem and restore them to full health and fellowship with himself. This is the boldness that our time, more than most, needs us to proclaim.

To Be with Jesus

Our association with Jesus will teach us, as it taught Peter and John, the deepest truths about ourselves and the highest truths about God. We need not be theologians or experienced in the ways of the world or longtime church members or leaders of the community or overly intelligent. We need only to be with Jesus—to associate with him in prayer and imitation. And as we do, people will wonder at our boldness as we live out in words and actions the truth of humanity and God as it is seen in Jesus Christ.

On Stewardship

Our Lord had a great deal to say about possessions; almost half of his parables are concerned with the wrong and right attitudes toward money, which is far from avoiding the topic. He talked about money more than most other subjects. There is not a word in his teaching that justifies the belittling of possessions. But he warned of the perils involved in getting money—in keeping, in hoarding. And he spoke of *giving* money. Always he stressed the importance of making money as a means to an end and not an end in itself. He recognized that it can be a great servant of humankind but that there is always a danger that it may become a person's master. Many have started out to get money and have found that money has gotten them.

The church has summarized its thinking on money under the word *stewardship*. Stewards are people who manage and take care of someone else's goods and possessions. They own nothing themselves. They work for someone else, making decisions and carrying out plans and programs in the best interests of the owner. That is what Jesus said we are: stewards. God is the owner. "The earth is the LORD's and the fulness thereof" (Psalm 24:1, RSV); in other words, everything that is, is God's. The natural world, the world of people, the world of things, the world of the spirit—the earth is the Lord's. Nothing that exists is exempt from the claim of God's ownership. And we are placed here as stewards of this earth. It is false and arrogant to say that any of it is our own. It has been put in trust to us. We have received it to enjoy it, to use it, to increase it, and to distribute it. But God is still the owner. We only manage *his* resources, taking care of the life and goods that *he* has given.

Holy Money

Money is holy. Not everyone believes that. Everyone thinks it is important, *quite* important. But not everyone is persuaded of the Christian and biblical conviction that money is holy.

Tithing is the ancient and biblical practice that puts into action the conviction that all money is holy. It is an offering of the firstfruits of our labor to the God who made this world of soil and rock, barley and grapes, silver and gold and tin—up to and including embossed plastic credit cards.

The tithe traditionally is a decision to offer God the first 10 percent of what we acquire through our labor. It is based on the conviction that we would have gotten nothing from all our sweat and exertion if God had not first given us ground to use, muscles to work, brains to think, and communities to live in and be employed in. We work with materials already given to us. We maintain our true relation to our work and its results when our first action is to give in the name of our Lord.

If we do not begin with giving—and giving substantially (10 percent is traditional and, for most of us, substantial)—we inevitably become dominated by the spirit of acquisition: getting and getting and *getting*. We become obsessed with keeping control of what we have. We scheme and covet. And in so doing, we profane our money. We violate the holiness of our money.

Money offered freely to Christ is given back to us changed in some deep and interior way. It can change us and the world around us. Generosity is our most reliable and useful means for turning what we have into a gift. The act of tithing is like leaven: all our money gets infected with the spirit of generosity and enjoyment. The tithe pulls all our possessions into lives of adoration and celebration.

But I must also warn you that the practice of tithing is dangerous. Jesus's angriest words were directed to scrupulous tithers. Tithing can subtly feed pride. It can create a snobbish elitism. It can fuel a censorious spirit that criticizes others. It can develop into self-righteousness that assumes that God is now obligated to take special notice.

On Keeping God to Ourselves

We can't keep God to ourselves. He is not a private acquisition.

It is God's nature to give of himself. If we are related to him truly, we participate in the sharing. We join the giving. The Christian is not a person who hides in a bunker but a person who explores all reality. When Christians keep to themselves what they ought to generously give, they deny the spirit and command of their Lord. Instead, we must celebrate the spreading light of Christ—the invasion of shadowlands with the brightness of saving love.

Of the absence of this love, journalist and social activist Dorothy Day once wrote, "I did not see anyone taking off his coat and giving it to the poor. I didn't see anyone having a banquet and calling in the lame, the halt, and the blind. . . . I wanted, though I did not know it then, a synthesis. I wanted life and I wanted the abundant life. I wanted it for others too."[*]

Later she did find it. She became a Christian. She went on to become one of the most effective apostles to the poor and oppressed that America has seen. She did it as an act of faith, through prayer and in love. She experienced the gift. In response, she gave. Will we?

[*] Dorothy Day, *The Long Loneliness: The Autobiography of Dorothy Day* (New York: Harper, 1952).

And the Tongue Is a Fire

The tongue is a small member, yet it boasts of great exploits.

How great a forest is set ablaze by a small fire! And the tongue is a fire.

James 3:5–6

Not long after we learn to speak the English language coherently, we realize that a surprising number of apparently grown-up people persist in using it to speak gibberish. Words are used with total disregard for their meanings. Sentences are constructed that are out of touch with reality. Speeches are made, sermons preached, books written, and television talks given that on examination turn out to be mainly nonsense.

No subject is exempt, but religion seems to me to get more than its fair share of this babble. Lies and blasphemies, ignorance and gossip, and malice and hypocrisy permeate discourse on God, sin, and salvation with dismaying regularity. There seems to be no regard for truth or consequences. Because these speakers and writers appear to be backed with evident wealth, carry themselves with confidence, and sound so sincere, a biblically uneducated public supposes that they know what they are talking about.

Truth is at risk in the world. If we think the wrong things about God, we are disoriented in reality. If we believe distorted presentations of the faith, our lives are deflected from God's best for us, our perceptions of life blurred. We want to get it right.

The first century was no better than this one in this regard. It was the pastoral task of James then, as it is mine now, to do something about it. Both how we speak and what we speak, especially when we are speaking about God, require solemn care. If we do it badly, we do great damage.

James pulled no punches: "The tongue is a fire" (3:6). He knew how important it is to use words well and how dangerous it is to use them badly. We need all the help we can get to learn the truth so that we will not be taken in by those who are false to the truth.

Do It Yourself

Many years ago in Baltimore, I heard Pete Seeger in concert. He played the five-string banjo and sang folk songs. I had never heard the banjo played like that before and was seized with the conviction that I had to learn to play the five-string banjo.

The next day, I went to the pawnshops on East Baltimore Street and found a banjo for seven dollars. I then went to the music shops around Peabody and found a used instruction book for five dollars. Picking and strumming, I set myself to learning how to play. (Some of those around me heard the unhappy results of my enthusiasm.)

My reason for being in Baltimore at the time was to study at Johns Hopkins University, preparing to be a teacher of Scripture. I remember thinking, *I hope that when I stand in a pulpit or at a lectern with the Scriptures in my hands that something similar will happen to the people who hear me as happened in me as I heard Pete Seeger: a fierce determination to read the Bible and enjoy it themselves.* The distinctive thing in that experience was not that I wanted to go back and hear *Pete Seeger* sing again but that I wanted to do it *myself.*

That is what pastors should want to take place when they teach and preach the Scriptures—not to have people become dependent on them but to have people become eager to get the Bible in their own hands and become competent in reading it.

The Complete Reader

Paul wrote to Timothy, "All scripture is inspired by God and profitable for teaching, for reproof, for correction, and for training in righteousness, that the man of God may be complete, equipped for every good work" (2 Timothy 3:16–17, RSV). The word *complete* (*artios*) means "skillfully put together"—not thrown together haphazardly but carefully crafted.

There are people in woodworking shops who compensate for their lack of skill in carpentry by using a lot of nails. And there are people lacking skill in living who try to keep their lives together with a lot of foreign matter: drugs, hobbies, money, diversions, and fads. But the skillful reading of Scripture is the means that God provides to put us together in the right way so that we are *complete*. It's what he uses to shape, correct, and train us as human beings with dignity and eternity rather than as conditioned consumers salivating at every commercial or as bundles of animal sensations enslaved to impulses of greed or lust or violence.

There are wrong ways to read Scripture, and Scripture is often read wrongly. Reading Scripture academically is only interesting. Reading Scripture superstitiously is merely silly. Scripture must be read *devoutly* so God's Word will craft us from the inside out, shaping our awkward, ill-formed lives until we are "complete, equipped for every good work."

When we read Scripture devoutly, we deepen and extend our involvement in the conversation that God has with us. We become more at home with his ways of working and more familiar with the way his mind works. When we read Scripture devoutly, we are listening to God speak to us. His Word addresses the centers of our beings and calls forth responses that complete our lives into wholeness.

Epiphany of Trouble

This statement took me so much by surprise that I can still remember it after twenty-seven years: "Do you know something? I have just realized that I like being in trouble. I am more myself when I am in trouble. I do things better." I can remember the exact place where the statement was made. My friend and I were coming out of a subway station at Fifty-Seventh Street in New York City. It was a summer night. I don't now remember what his particular trouble was, only his statement about the effect it had on him.

Since then, I have kept my eyes and ears open. Most people are not as ingenuously honest as my friend during that little epiphany, but I am convinced that many share his preference. A crisis gives us the stimulus to live at our best. Trouble forces us to gather our energy. We are standing around bored, wondering what to do with our lives, and then something takes place (war, accident, death, rejection, or danger) that removes all the ambiguity and wipes out the boredom. Then suddenly we are alert and excited—alive.

God is commonly understood as the extra help we need to deal with the trouble in our lives: sickness, loss, disappointment, failure, or guilt. There is no question but that he is—Christ began his work in acts of healing, helping, and delivering. But after we are healed, what do we do? After we are forgiven, what do we do?

Let me put this in personal terms as your pastor. When someone is sick, I know what to do. When there is a death in someone's family, I know what to do. When someone comes to me with a sense of guilt, I know what to do. But most of you most of the time are not sick or grieving or failing. Most of the congregation, most of the time, is getting on fairly well, thank you. They're getting to work on time, making the mortgage payments, staying on speaking terms with the neighbors, and eating three fairly decent meals a day. What do I do with you during these times? Do I wait around for the next emergency? Maybe if I do a really good job on Sundays teaching you the moral discipline so that you will stay out of trouble, I won't have to work so hard during the week! Or is there something else?

Many people find a decent, comfortable life like that intolerable, so they create trouble just to keep the action going. They quarrel or they get sick or they precipitate an accident. Then they are not bored anymore. Then they have a reason for living. There is pain in that, of course, but the pain is preferable to the meaningless routine. I heard once that one of the startling things found in a study of Great Britain during World War II was that during the Nazi bombing of London, nearly all the citizens' psychological neuroses disappeared. People didn't have time to be emotionally disturbed; they were in deadly trouble, and they had to do something about it.[*]

I also once heard an amusing but apparently true story of a woman who was paralyzed and couldn't leave her bed. She was wealthy and could command physicians and counselors to come to her. Nothing helped. Her condition became a great puzzle to her physician and psychiatrist. One day in despera-

***

[*] This anecdote should not be taken as a wide dismissal of mental health conditions or treatments by Eugene, who deeply respected the unique contributions of psychology and clinical counseling and encouraged Christians to do the same. His point in context is to discourage a kind of codependency sometimes found in Christian preaching. After all, if faith is founded as merely a response to spiritual crisis, how genuine can it be in the everyday?

tion, the physician and psychiatrist conspired to bring about her healing. They had a friend make a fire in a safe place, which sent out great billows of smoke through the house, and then yell, "Fire! Fire!" The two doctors were in the room with the woman at the time and ran out as if for their lives, leaving her helpless in the bed behind them, and waited outside. In a few minutes, she came running out after them.

Surely a terrible practice! But there are preachers who do that too. They yell fire and brimstone to mobilize in people the healthy response of repentance. And, of course, it works—some of the time. The problem is that I have to come back to this pulpit every week. And while it is true that we are living in crisis all the time, that we do not know the hour of our death, and that judgment may intervene at the least expected time, there is far more to life than dealing with crises.

But here is the question: How do we live at our best when we don't have to?

Entering Salvation

What is Jesus up to? What are his intentions? What is he planning? In a word, *salvation*.

Do we think we know what this word *salvation* means? It is so common in our language, especially in our religious language, that it is a cliché. But it refers to action that exceeds our comprehension even as it invites our participation. We need to return to the word with fresh attention, with lively curiosity, over and over again, and discover anew the central action of the universe. Jesus is ready to save.

He says many true things, and he does many right things. But his hidden (or not-so-hidden) agenda that gives order and goal to all the details is salvation. The consequence for us who name the name of Jesus and who assemble regularly to worship him is that we must be prepared to enter into his act of salvation.

We cannot take a word of Jesus here and think on it for a few minutes, then admire an act there. This is a world-determining and life-transforming person we are involved with. No detail of our lives is exempt from his energetic, eternal work.

Personal Best

My first and continuing pastoral purpose in this pulpit is that you confess Christ personally. As a pastor, I have never wanted to be a moral policeman. Your morals are not that interesting to me. I am not interested in rewarding you when you are good or punishing you when you are bad, nor as a pastor have I wanted to gather large crowds here for religious entertainment. It makes little difference to me whether there are many or few in this place. Religious crowds are the easiest crowds to gather. But increasing the number of people under one roof has never been a conspicuously successful way of involving people in what is essential. The pastoral act that is central for me is to introduce God at his personal best (Jesus, the Christ) to human beings at their personal best.

That is exactly what I hope happens here each week. I don't want merely to tell you about this great story I have been reading in this book (the Bible); I want you to meet the Author. And he has told me that he wants to meet *you*—to involve you in a new story he is making. I can arrange the interview.

Do you see why I have little interest in entertaining you with gossip about God? Do you see why I have little interest in lecturing you about what kind of life you ought to lead? There is something far more interesting and more to the point about introducing you personally to the personal God so that you no longer talk *about* God but *to* him. I long for you to confess Christ personally and get in on the new creative work that God is writing: the story of your salvation.

If I Get Caught Up,
Who Will Be Your Pastor?

It is not obvious what pastors do—at least it is not obvious to me. So I keep asking myself, *What am I doing here? What do I want to do?*

What I want to do is say the name *God* accurately so that you will know the basic reality of your existence and know what's going on. And I want to say that name *personally,* alongside and with you in the actual circumstances of your lives, so that you will recognize and respond to the God who is both on your side and at your side when it doesn't seem like it—when you don't feel as though it's true.

Why do I have such a difficult time keeping this focus? Why am I so easily distracted? One reason is that I am asked to do many things other than this, most of which seem useful and important. The world of religion generates a huge market for meeting all the needs that don't get met in the shopping mall. Pastors are conspicuous in this religious marketplace and are expected to come up with "products" that give "customer satisfaction."

The needs seem legitimate enough, and since I am the one being asked, I fall into the practice of merchandising moral advice and religious comfort. Before long, I find that I am the program director of a flourishing business. I spend my time figuring out ways to attractively display God-products. I become skilled at pleasing the customers. Before I realize what has happened, the mystery and love and majesty of God are obliterated by the noise and frenzy of the religious marketplace.

But then, who will say the name *God* in such a way that the community can see him for who he is, our Lord and Savior, and not something neatly packaged and priced to meet our consumer needs? And who will have the time to stand with you in the places of confusion and darkness and hurt long enough to discern the healing and salvation being worked out behind the scenes, under the surface?

If I get all caught up in running the store, who will be your pastor?

Getting Out the News

*E*vangelism is the label we give to all those words and gestures, acts of witness both deliberate and subconscious, that get out the news in a personal way that God is alive in the world, that it is his will that we experience his love, and that Jesus Christ provides the way in which we get in on it. *Saved* is the usual term for it.

Many people don't understand this good news. They don't know that God is *for* them. And they don't know the way and are wasting their lives hunting and pecking, guessing and groping, hoping that they will get lucky someday with a lottery ticket to heaven. But as Christians, we know that God is for us and know the way to receive him in Jesus. We don't know everything about these great issues, but we know at least that much. And we know that it is both our obligation and our joy to tell others.

G. K. Chesterton once turned a well-known aphorism on its head: "If a thing is worth doing, it is worth doing badly."[*] I think of that in regard to evangelism. Not many of us think of ourselves as experts in it. Mostly we are aware of our omissions, our missed opportunities, and our negligence. We sometimes associate the action of evangelism with football-stadium crowds and television glamour.

---

[*] G. K. Chesterton, *What's Wrong with the World,* part 4, chapter 14, www .gutenberg.org/files/1717/1717-h/1717-h.htm; see also "A Thing Worth Doing," *The Apostolate of Common Sense* (blog), April 29, 2012, www.chesterton.org /a-thing-worth-doing/.

But most evangelism is incremental and unobtrusive. Most evangelism takes place in the world as Christians live and work alongside one another in families and at jobs over the course of ten and twenty and thirty years. The primary field for evangelism is not with strangers who cross our lives briefly but with the people with whom we live and work and socialize over a lifetime. That is why it is so difficult—we must learn how to communicate through the ordinariness of our lives the extraordinariness of God's grace. We need constant stimuli and direction in both what to say and how to say it right with our words and our lives.

Still, it takes place. The news is getting out.

PART THREE

On Prayers and Praises

Everything GOD does is right—
    the trademark on all his works is
    love.
GOD's there, listening for all who
    pray,
    for all who pray and mean it. . . .
My mouth is filled with GOD's praise.
    Let everything living bless him,
    bless his holy name from now to
    eternity!

Psalm 145:17–18, 21, MSG

On the Nature of a Congregation

A Christian congregation is a group of people who decide, together, to pay attention.

Getting the Story Straight

Christian life begins as something simple and clean: God and ourselves. It doesn't stay that way. Clutter crowds us. Pollution messes us up. We lose our way and get frantic. We get tired and wonder if this is all there is to it.

Then we come together as a community. We worship God and greet each other. As we do this, we get the story straight again about the God who makes us, the Christ who saves us, and the Spirit who works in us to repeat our Lord's words and deeds among our neighbors in the world.

In spiritual community, we work to recover the true story and identity of each of us, in which we realize our dignity and beauty and find out how to love. We must keep that basic and plain: as little of us as possible and as much of God as we can take in.

Gospel Sensuality

The gospel of Jesus Christ is shockingly sensual. Every physical sense we possess is brought into play to receive and express the new life. Jesus does not distill the raw material of flesh and earth into a fine and rarified spirit. He returns us to the physical; he immerses us in materiality. The God who created rocks, trees, torsos, and tongues and became flesh in Jesus Christ recovers and redeems our five senses in the practice of faith, love, and hope.

There is much in the life of faith that is inaccessible to our senses. We cannot see God, we cannot handle the Spirit, and we cannot hear the angels. But there is an astonishing sensuality nevertheless: baptismal waters, Eucharistic bread and wine, and anointing oil. "Taste and see" was the urgent invitation of one psalmist (Psalm 34:8).

Jesus spent much of his time touching and being touched, speaking and listening, seeing and being seen. He not only forgave sins (an interior, nonsensory operation) but also restored sight and speech and hearing and recovered the use of arms and legs so that men and women could live the faith in their hearts as well as with their bodies. Senses dulled by sin are sharpened in holiness. The body of Jesus was the means by which the life of God was experienced and expressed in revelation to us; our bodies are also the means by which the life of God is experienced and expressed in faith.

As Jesus teaches us what is going on in this new life that God creates and develops in us, he often uses the experience of our senses to inform our minds: the taste of salt, for instance, and the phenomenon of light. We become more physical, not less, as we become and mature as Christians. Our physical capacities and the exercise of our senses make it possible for us and for those around us to experience God, who revealed himself in the flesh of Jesus.

Sharpened Pilgrims

Christians through the centuries have gone on pilgrimages to restore sharpness to vision that has become blurred by habit and familiarity. A life of faith in Christ is, above all, an immersion in events and facts, in the concrete, hard-edged features of rocks and swords, in the awareness-shaping forces of scenery and weather.

When words like *love, Jesus, sin, Peter, grace,* and *Spirit* are reduced to only dictionary entries or seen as merely subjects to discuss and explain, they no longer matter to the way we live our lives, are no longer elements in the great energies that shape our salvation.

Unwashed Holiness

Eight sandwiches (four tuna fish and four peanut butter), a bag of Lambert cherries, two water bottles, and a few cookies were in my daypack, and we anticipated a bountifully provisioned lunch in a few hours. Grinnell Glacier, our destination, was visible on the side of a mountain five miles away. I was in the company of good friends and feeling the fullness of life, the exuberant goodness of the health and beauty that I was stepping into for the next few hours. Standing at the trailhead, I said to my friend, "I love these moments—poised at a trailhead, about to start into an alpine hike. It is exactly the way I feel every Sunday morning when I enter the sanctuary and call my friends to worship our Lord."

Anticipation. Energy focused and effortless. God. Stepping into unwashed holiness. Every time I set out on a mountain hike and every time I enter into worship at Christ Our King, the feeling is there again, fresh and clean.

Worship is a trailhead that leads us into the heightened attentiveness and adoration that is worship of God. Like Montana air, it renews. Like being immersed in solitude and silence—the elemental mountains and wind, sun and water—it restores. This unwashed, holy life can prepare us to experience the other set of elementals: the Word and sacraments, songs and prayers, greetings and blessings that we plunge into every time we worship the God revealed in Jesus Christ.

First Steps

A key conviction in the Christian way is "the priesthood of all believers"—that each person can be a priest to the other, with each of us mediating grace, mercy, and forgiveness, and with each of us capable of connecting with another in a way that brings God's love home with personal force. The contemporary implications of that conviction can, perhaps, be better realized by renaming it "the *leadership* of all believers."

Leadership is that capacity everyone has for taking the first step, making it possible for others to follow—the capacity to connect with another so that others can get in on what we are in on. What we are "in on" is Christ.

The Foundational Consequence

God speaks to us. This is the great foundational fact of our faith. God speaks *to us,* and his speaking brings us into existence and into salvation. Language is the means by which what is unknown becomes known and what is hidden becomes accessible.

God uses language to bring into being his will. His will is now evident to us in trees and skies and azaleas, in baptisms and praises, in conversions and Eucharist, in love and mercy. We see and hear it all around us, these consequences of God's speaking. And in return, we speak to God. This is the great foundational consequence of our faith. We speak to God, and our speaking brings into the open his glory, our assent to his creating and saving Word, and our sheer and exultant *joy* in him.

Language—this wonderful gift, this mysterious capacity that we have to say who we are, to bring out into the open the secrets of our hearts, the nuances of our emotions, and the thoughts whether confused or clear in our minds—is our basic means for working out who we are by answering God, responding to his invitations and commands.

The Great Invisibles

Worship centers our life. In worship, we let God have the first word. We set the mood of days to come by practicing adoration and praise. We establish a sense of reality in which the "great invisibles" (God, Christ, and Spirit) can be as fresh and present to us in daily life as our family members and workplaces and job lists.

Fragments of Worship

The fragments of our lives find an inner coherence in the act of worship. The contrasts and diversities among us that sometimes seem like chaos are centered when we assemble as God's community in worship. Our worship restores us to a wholeness that keeps us sane in the midst of bedlam, joyous in the face of doom.

The Backward Word

When the perishable is lost in the imperishable, the mortal lost in the immortal, this saying will come true: "Death is swallowed up in victory" "O death, where is your sting? O Hades, where is your victory?"

1 Corinthians 15:54, PHILLIPS

The world gives us a bad education: words are turned backward, mispronounced, distorted, badly constructed, and ruined in clichés. *Live* spelled backward is *evil*. Evil captured the headlines in Jerusalem two thousand years ago, and it captures them still. But it is the live Jesus who has captured history—and captures us.

All the elements that make up life, like the letters that make up the alphabet, can be used against their purpose. They can be used to confuse, to lie, and to destroy. They are reversed and perverted by cruelty and mockery, sin and death.

But then, unaccountably, in the silence of the tomb, past the mysteries of death, they are rearranged and put straight. The basic word is spelled right before us in Jesus raised, alive. Saint Paul, in his dazzling resurrection meditation in 1 Corinthians 15, contrasts resurrection with vanity, fullness with emptiness, reality with illusion, live with evil. All his superlatives are understatements. Jesus breaks the spell of the reversed, backward spoken word.

Jesus's resurrection spells the words right so that we can speak rightly, sing in tune, and live saved. *Live,* not *evil,* is the way to spell it. Resurrection recovers the original word, the Word become flesh, the cursed word that by reversing the letters was turned into a blasphemous parody of itself. The same resurrection recovers the meaning to our speech, gives sense to our action.

And an eternal purpose to our lives.

The Vision Shows Us

God's world is always larger than our world. The vision shows us how large. The Christian faith must never be restricted to what we are comfortable with: taking care of only ourselves. We are in on something large.

Without the vision, the world becomes small and selfish. With the vision, the world becomes large and generous. And our lives collect, they accumulate, and they become community and church. Without the vision, our church reduces itself to repetitious programs and rituals. Without the vision, our church looks at people as customers who help us pay the bills and put on the programs.

On Growing from the Roots

Christian growth, like any kind of growth, needs to be in continuous touch with the sources of its nourishment. If it develops more activity than its roots can support, it loses productivity. If it initiates activity that has no basis in its roots, it will wither quickly, to be replaced the next week by another cut-flower fad.

On Light

L ight is a symbol, both common and central among Christians—a symbol for Christ.

As light pours into our lives from the sun, so Christ's love warms and illuminates us in mercy and grace. The light that is Christ reaches into all that is our world. It also reaches into all that is the person.

The world is shown to be a world that God loves; the person is shown to be a creature whom God saves. This is the great epiphany: Christ enlightens everything and everyone, draws our fragmented and shadowed lives into an experienced wholeness.

Interior Experts

There is nothing more important for a pastor to do than teach people how to pray.

Don't misunderstand. I don't mean "to say your prayers better." I am not interested in lectures on prayer. The term *prayer* refers to the cultivation of your interior self, the experienced practice of God's presence in the entirety of your life, not just the "religious" parts.

In prayer, we deal with our most ordinary self, everybody's ordinary self, and learn to answer in the simplest and most direct language the God who speaks to us.

We have many people all around us who show us how to deal with the exterior parts of our lives, and we get very good at it. But we must learn how to deal with the interior of our lives and become experts in it. I don't want you to hunt and peck for the rest of your life, always feeling inadequate, forever apologizing for your ineptness. I want you to get good at prayer.

Little Prayer

One of the indignities to which pastors are routinely subjected is being asked by well-meaning strangers, "Say a little prayer for us, will you?"

Someday, when I get courage, I am going to roar, "I will not! 'Little prayer' indeed! Do you not realize that in prayer we approach the awesome, holy God? Attend to the fiery center of all existence? And 'say a little prayer'? Do you think prayer is recitation—saying a piece before classmates and parents for their amusement? Do you not know that prayer is our most inward, intimate speech, fashioned out of our deepest longings and often lapsing into inarticulate groaning?"

But if I remain timid among unwary strangers, I am at least free to tell you, my friends who commit yourselves to live by faith in Jesus Christ, that among the essential requirements of this life is that we pray in the Spirit ardently. Prayer is not devotional background patter (like that dreadful canned music in eating establishments) that soothes tense nerves and covers up the incidental noise of life. The premise of prayer is that we are spoken to by God. He calls us into being by his Word and leads us into personal relationship by his Word.

What is the normal response of a person spoken to? Is it not to reply? Prayer is the reply. It is answering speech. God's Word addresses us at the very center of our beings—at our essential creation, in our deepest longings, regarding our ultimate destinies. We answer: We praise, we confess, we question, we adore, we doubt, and we promise. We pray. These answering words are evoked from our depths. They cover the entire range of our beings. They can be spoken in any mood with the exception of the frivolous. They can deal with anything, but not with what we don't care about.

James brings the most practical letter in the New Testament to its most practical conclusion by providing two insights that train us to pray in the Spirit ardently (see 5:13–18). "Is any one among you suffering? Let him pray" (verse 13, RSV). Prayer is the first thing we do, not the second, not the third, not the last. We commonly think of prayer as a court of last resort, what we do when we have exhausted our own resources and things still don't work. But prayer is not trying to get God to do what we can't do ourselves; it is getting in on what God is already doing.

Prayer is, remember, *answering* speech. God has the first word. We don't drag God into our conversation; God invites us into his. "Is any one among you suffering?" Is there trouble anywhere? Is there a sense of loss, inadequacy, or bewilderment? Find out what God is saying, enter the conversation, and get in on the action at that point. "Eli'jah was a man of like nature with ourselves and he prayed" (verse 17, RSV). Anyone can pray. Prayer is not for the experts. Prayer is not for the few with aptitudes for piety. You don't have to be a saint to pray. You don't even have to be a Christian. If you are "like" everybody else, you can pray. It is, again, answering speech.

We don't make up an original address and present it to the Almighty. We simply answer.

Prayer from the Center

Prayer is the activity that I am convinced is most human and humanizing. Sometimes, the following request is made of me: "Pastor, teach me to pray." When it comes, I am happy, for I know that I now have a companion in praying, that another friend is ready to enter this research laboratory of the spirit where the original work of discovering and participating in God's grace takes place. I want to be a pastor who prays, a pastor to whom you freely and unhesitatingly bring requests for prayer.

But I also want a congregation who prays, a congregation whom I can ask to pray for me and others, a people who are acquiring confidence in working out of the center, the God-center of mercy and healing and grace.

That is what prayer is: the action that starts at the God-center and works out from that. It is the major task we have as pastors and people: to acquire facility in working from the interior center to the exterior periphery. We get a lot of schooling and stimuli to work on in the outside world of animals and things; my passion is that we acquire an equivalent facility in the inside world of being and spirit.

The Meeting

God comes to us; we come to God; the meeting is salvation. We celebrate this meeting in our acts of worship. Worship directs us and tells us that God's coming and our coming result in real meeting, not simply an appearance of it.

Worship heightens our awareness so that we can become conscious of the eternal intersections that take place in our hearts when God's grace connects with our groping faith.

Worship intensifies joy as the Word of God is spoken clearly and the voices of praise are harmonized in being and coordinated in affirmation.

A New Label

Paul, an apostle of Christ Jesus by the will of God,
   To the saints who are also faithful in Christ Jesus:
   Grace to you and peace from God our Father and the
Lord Jesus Christ.

Ephesians 1:1–2, RSV

Paul calls us saints. It stands as one of the most extravagant uses of language ever. Does he mean it? Does he know us at all? Or is this cynical sales-pitch flattery? We've been called many things during our lifetimes, but never this—at least not by the people who know us. What's going on here?

Saints. Saint Paul calls us saints. We're used to being categorized intellectually (underachiever, average, gifted and talented), psychologically (introvert, extrovert), socially (lower-, middle-, upper-class), by size (short, medium, tall), by weight (underweight, average weight, overweight), and by law (guilty, acquitted). But this is a new label. It takes some getting used to.

Our usual labels direct attention to what we can expect from each other; this one directs attention to what we can expect from God. *Saint* doesn't name what we do or can do; it names what God has done and does—in us.

Praying Toward the Center

Prayer is the act that pulls us into the center of what it means to be ourselves.

In praying, we are becoming most human.

The Responsibility of Words

Words. Syllables. Sentences.

We use words so commonly and so easily that we lose touch with how marvelous and precious they are. We have capacity to speak words and make ourselves understood and capacity to listen to words and understand another. The simple (or complex!) fact that we can speak words does not guarantee that we will speak them well—or speak the truth. We can, and do, speak nonsense. We can, and do, tell lies.

Words delight us so much because they bring us into understanding relations with the world and into intimate relations with people, but words can also dismay us, even destroy us, as they misrepresent or falsify or manipulate. Because words are so basic to who we are and the way the world is and who God is and the way he comes to us and because words are so commonly reduced in value and so easily misused, the church takes a few of its members aside as preachers and teachers and puts them, so to speak, in charge of the words.

"Your task," the church says on these occasions, "is to make sure we hear and listen to these words. If we forget or devalue these words, we are going to miss the point of everything. We are going to miss God. There is a lot going on. There are things to do and places to go and people to meet. There are babies to change and payrolls to meet, meals to prepare and cars to repair, wounds to heal and problems to solve. In the crises and the challenges, the noise and the frenzy of all this, we need someone who will faithfully and accurately say the Word, proclaim the Word, teach the Word—and stay with us as we listen and pray and believe it."

Can There Be Conversation?

Do not say, "I am only a youth";
for to all to whom I send you you shall go,
and whatever I command you you shall speak.

Jeremiah 1:7, RSV

Can there be conversation between a God who speaks worlds into being and speaks our lives into being and those of us who use words to get a second helping of potatoes or to tell a checkout clerk that we were overcharged $3.50 on some broccoli? Are these words compatible? Aren't we dealing with two completely different orders of magnitude?

We might have no doubt about the validity of God's words, but we might not think *our* words are valid in the same way. We might think our words are not worthy of being entered into a conversation with God. But what we do not see is that our sense of unworthiness is initiating a conversation. In the very act of excluding ourselves, we have begun to include ourselves in a dialogue—by answering God.

When our words and God's words are joined, something new starts to happen. Our words are validated. They become authenticated. They function for the exact reason God's words function: to reveal and create. So says the Lord to Jeremiah, "Do not denigrate yourself with, 'I am only a youth';

you have words, you will speak, and that is enough." At least part of what it means to be in the image of God is to have language—to be able to speak and listen to words that link these mysterious interiors of our lives in love and under-standing.

Prayer Companion

Hear my cry, O God;
  listen to my prayer.
From the end of the earth I call to you,
  when my heart is faint.
Lead me to the rock
  that is higher than I.

Psalm 61:1–2

For us who have accepted Christ as our Lord and Savior, which is the fundamental commitment of our lives to the God who loves us and commits himself to us in Jesus, prayer is the most comprehensive and essential of actions.

In this work, we deliberately develop every part of our lives, body and soul, in response to God rather than to the stimuli that bombard us from the world. It is hard, exacting work—this life of prayer—but not at all grim. Not infrequently, geysers of spontaneous joy erupt and spray out goodness. This praying life is a lifelong task in which we need each other's companionship.

The best companion I know in this, after our Lord himself, is David. Read his psalms. They are David assembling all his experiences, all his difficulties and achievements, and all his doubts and affirmations before God and finding them shaped into wholeness, into salvation—as he becomes more honestly himself and more God's, both at the same time. Much, we can hope, like us.

On Joy at Church

More praising goes on in church, more joy is expressed in the context of the Christian congregation, than anywhere else on the face of the earth.

Think through the places you spent time this week. The supermarkets and the department stores are grim places, by and large. People pushing their food baskets, anxiously comparing prices, complaints etched into their faces as they pay the clerks. Not a happy environment. The roads you drive on? Worried, compulsive people are behind the wheels of most of those cars. If you should wait too long after a light has changed, if you should diverge a little from your lane, what will the reaction be? Angry horn blowing, scowls, rude looks. The highway is not a very joyful place. The automobile display room and the used-car lot: I see many people milling around there, but the joy and anticipation of getting another car are subordinated to the suspicion and shrewdness of making a deal. The athletic event: there are extravagant emotional expressions there, but it is surprising how few of them are joyful. The dominant mood is complaining, arguing, and criticizing.

I would be willing to match the church against any of these places as a context for joy and praise. I know it's not a perfect place. I know it could be improved. I know that some people are disappointed in it. But I don't find any other place in the world where there is such a consistent friendliness, such a steady joy, such a relaxed rejoicing in God's love. There is more generosity when it comes to money in church than anywhere I know. Where else in this community can you find people giving their money away each week, then standing up and singing, "Praise God from whom all blessings flow"? Have you ever been to the supermarket and had some stranger walk up to you and ask, "Say, you're new here, aren't you? I'd like to know you better." But it happens among us Christians all the time.

I know the other side of this. I know there are people in every church who harbor ill feelings for each other. I know some are so hurt and crushed by life that they feel they can't express any joy. I know some sit through services with dullness and apathy—indifferent. I know all that, better than any of you perhaps. And I don't deny or minimize it.

What I do say is that despite all of it, perhaps *because* of it, there is more praise, more celebration, and more joy found in the church than anywhere else in the world.

On Adequacy and Abundance

We come to the communion table responding to God's invitation: we reaffirm, reexperience, remember, and receive.

We *all* are called. We *each* are served. Commonly. Individually. Our commonness is emphasized; our uniqueness is preserved. We get our basic needs met adequately; we receive the completion of our aspirations abundantly.

Christian faith is survival—bread. But is it not also exuberance—wine? God gives us life eternal. On every continent and in every nation, Christians receive this life.

On Happiness

For a while, our country was plastered with happy faces—those bright-yellow moon faces with infectious grins on them. In those days, it seemed, smiles were in. It was chic to be happy. The happy face had gone commercial, and if you couldn't quite manage to put one on your own face, you could buy one and stick it on your car bumper or buy a dress or shirt whose pattern would advertise your good cheer.

I like happy faces. Who doesn't? If you have your choice between a smile and a frown, who wouldn't choose the smile? It brightens the landscape. It lifts the spirits. I have gotten so attached to the happy face that I feel that there is something almost unpatriotic—or at least unchristian—in being sad. The darker moods of the human personality have largely been banished. They simply aren't good for business anymore.

But for all the popularity of happiness, it is a myth that the Christian always wears a smile. There is a stream of joy that runs through the Christian life and keeps surfacing in praise and glad service. There is a powerful note of celebration in the church's life and the Christian's witness. But that is not the kind of smile that maintains itself by ignoring or denying everything that is troubling or difficult.

As Christians who face existence with God's Word and his will, we're going to come upon difficult situations. We must wrestle with unanswerable questions. If we take seriously the commands of God and give ourselves seriously to the task of loving our neighbors and our enemies, we are going to find ourselves in conflict with others, even find ourselves looking silly and naive—a laughingstock, in short. And that is not pleasant. We are going to be plunged into feelings of despair when we think that God is unfair. We will sometimes feel that there is no justice in God's world or even that we have been played for suckers.

When many people enter such dark tunnels, they first think, *If only I were a better Christian, I wouldn't feel this way. If I just had more faith, these blasphemous thoughts would never cross my mind. If only I could be well balanced and peaceful and accepting of God's will in my life, like the really good Christians!*

But the Christian is not the one who never has these doubts or feelings of despair. The Christian is the one who believes in spite of them, who does God's command even when he doesn't feel like it, who hopes when there is nothing to hope for.

The picture we have of Jesus in the Garden of Gethsemane shows him agonizing over the decision of the Cross. He struggled with his own feelings. He wrestled with the will of God and finally chose the will of God. And out of this struggle came something we call good news.

The Reality of Worship

When we worship God, we discover how his blessings shape our lives. We also discover how to bless and be blessed by our neighbors' lives.

In worship, God becomes more real to us. But the mystery is this: so do our neighbors.

Existence Illuminated

The Psalms give us access to an environment in which God is the pivotal center of life and everything else is peripheral. All other people, events, and circumstances in our lives become third parties. Existence—*all of it*—is suddenly illuminated in direct relationship to God himself.

Neither bane nor blessing distracts the psalmist from this center. He is not misled by demons of size, influence, importance, or power. He turns his back on the gaudy pantheons of Canaan and Assyria and gives himself to personal intensities that become awe and intimacy before God.

For such reasons, among people who want to pray, the Psalms are God's best gifts. By them, we can see.

Honesty in Worship

Honesty in worship is maintained by keeping in touch with other Christians in company before God. There are no instances that we know of when Christians have successfully severed themselves from a regular gathering in community. There is no evidence that worship is an option, a kind of frill that you add on if you feel like it and omit if you don't.

Community worship keeps our relationships with God from depending on our feelings (our feelings are notorious deceivers) and restrains us from indulging in private, quirky, and self-righteous hobbies. It keeps us connected to the whole revelation in the whole company of all God's people. Thus, we worship in truth.

The Word and Sacraments

*Adapted from a sermon Eugene preached at
the ordination of a new pastor*

The reason pastors are ordained to the church's ministry of the Word and sacraments is that we, the people who have dared to believe that Jesus Christ is Lord and Savior, need help in keeping our beliefs sharp and accurate and intact.

We don't trust ourselves—our emotions seduce us to infidelities. We know that we are launched on a difficult and dangerous act of faith and that strong influences are intent on diluting or destroying it. We want you to give us help. Be a pastor, a minister of the Word and sacraments, in the middle of this world's life. Be a minister of the Word and sacraments to us in all the different parts and stages of our lives: in our work and play, with our children and our parents, at birth and death, in our celebrations and sorrows, on those days when morning breaks over us in a wash of sunshine, and on those other days that are all drizzle. This isn't the only task in the life of faith, but it is the *pastor's* task. We will find someone else to do the other important and essential tasks. This is yours: the Word and sacraments.

We are going to ordain you to this ministry, and we want your vow that you will stick to it. This is not a temporary job assignment but a way of life that we need lived out in our community. We know you are launched on the same difficult belief venture, in the same dangerous world that we are. We know your emotions are as fickle as ours and that your mind can play the same tricks on you as ours do on us. That is why we are going to ordain and install you and why we are going to exact a vow from you. We know there will be days and months, maybe even years, when we won't feel as though we are believing anything and won't want to hear it from you. And we know there will be days and weeks and maybe even years when you won't feel like saying it. It doesn't matter. Do it. You are ordained to this. It will not be optional. You will be vowed to it.

There may be times when we come as a committee or a delegation and demand that you tell us something else, something other than what we are telling you now. Promise right now that you won't give in to what we demand of you. You are not the minister of our changing desires or our time-conditioned understanding of our needs or secularized hopes for something better.

With these vows of ordination, we are binding you fast to the mast of the Word and sacraments so that you will be unable to respond to the Siren voices.* There are many other things to be done in this wrecked world, and we are going to be doing at least some of them. But if we don't know the basic terms with which we are working, the foundational realities with which we are dealing—God, kingdom, and gospel—we are going to end up living futile fantasy lives. Your task is to keep telling the basic story, representing the presence of the Spirit, insisting on the priority of God, and speaking the biblical words of command and promise and invitation.

---

* Eugene is alluding to Odysseus's instructions to his sailors in Homer's *Odyssey* for entering the dangerous waters haunted by the tempting and deadly Sirens who sought to lure sailors to leave the ship and drown.

The Spectator and
the Death of Worship

The spectator is the death of worship. The person who comes to be diverted or amused does not worship. Worship is response—*heartily*.

Heart in biblical language is the center of our personalities. It is where what is most uniquely *us* originates. *Heartily* does not mean noisily or conspicuously but rather decently, inwardly, *personally*.

I read once—it might have been in Søren Kierkegaard—that many people who engage in acts of worship mistakenly think they are watching performances. Whoever said it, this is true. They sit back and expect the pastor and choir to make them feel religious. They then criticize or applaud or sleep, as is the practice of theatergoers who have paid the price of admission. But that is not the way it is.

When we worship, the stage is eternity and we are on it. The audience is God. Every worshipper is before God, and in the silence, we speak from our hearts to the God who speaks to us.

The Habit of Faith

"Nothing," someone once observed, "is quite so temporary as a bath." Just as the cleanliness of our bodies needs repeated and frequent attention, so does the vitality of our faith. Left to themselves, hands become dirty, signposts become dull, and our faith loses its luster.

One of the major tasks of a community of faith is to prevent Christianity from becoming a dull habit. Each weekly act of worship can become a fresh coming to God, prompting a new readiness to listen to his Word, inviting us each into an audacious and unprecedented venture in faith and obedience. Christian faith should not be a predictable routine but rather a passionate response to our Lord the Spirit, who provides gifts for new acts of love, creative decisions in forgiveness, and stirring innovations of hope.

Here is the truth: we cannot live on the leftovers from last month's Lord's Supper or on the interest from last year's deposit of faith. Each time we truly worship, we are asking our Lord to take the materials of our lives and reform them into a new discipleship. Our worship is an act of expectation that prevents our faith from petrifying into self-righteousness or our praise from becoming arthritic from disuse.

The Good News of Giving

I learned the importance of money in the church when I preached once in a Dutch Reformed church on Long Island. I was a theology student in a strange setting, and I was nervous. I led worship and gave my sermon. As I spoke, six men stood across the back of the sanctuary with their arms folded and glowered at me. The longer I preached, the angrier they became. I could not connect what I was saying in my sermon with the disapproval of those angry Dutchmen.

I pronounced the benediction and went to the door. The leader of the six delivered his blunt reprimand: "You forgot to take up the offering." I have never forgotten to do it since. I learned my lesson. Money is enormously important in the church. But those Dutchmen also had something to learn: giving money is an incredibly *joyful* act. In church, the facts of money and the spirit of generosity are interfused.

No one has so thoroughly connected the importance of money with the joy of giving as Saint Paul: "Each of you must give as you have made up your mind, not reluctantly or under compulsion, for God loves a cheerful giver" (2 Corinthians 9:7). Very early, I made the determination that I would never be a money raiser in the church. Fundraising is not pastoral work; it contradicts the spirit of the gospel of grace. But I also realized at the outset of my ministry that it is imperative that I proclaim the good news of giving. Why? Because we Christians ought to generously enjoy the rich materiality of the gospel.

The gospel of Jesus Christ is the most materialistic religion the world has seen. Biblical religion is saturated in the material, in the flesh, in *things*. But to delight in materiality the way God does means to handle it the way he handles it, which is by generously giving, not stingily gripping.

Giving, the Style of the Universe

How much is generous? There is no rule, but there is guidance: biblical guidance is the tithe. Ten percent off the top. It is not what we pay to be good; it is that disciplined use of our money that trains us in generosity and therefore in *enjoyment* of all materiality. By careful planning, all of us (rich or poor) within two or three years can be giving a tithe—some of us far more.

Generosity means dealing with our greed and our impulsive self-indulgences. It means reordering priorities and values. Most people's lack of generosity is due not to money problems but to greed problems, avarice problems, *value* problems. The tithe is wise guidance for learning to give our money generously.

Giving is the style of the universe. Giving is woven into the fabric of existence. If we try to live by getting instead of giving, we go against the stream. It is like going against the law of gravity: the result is bruises and broken bones. We see many people tightly holding on to their money, miserable in their fearful avarice. But have you ever seen a tight-lipped, anxiety-ridden *generous* person?

All life is given. It must continue to be given to stay true to its nature. "God so loved the world that he *gave*" (John 3:16). Giving is the way the world is. God gives away everything that is. When we give our money, we begin to do, clumsily and awkwardly at first, what God does expertly.

On the Bottom Line

What will it profit them if they gain the whole world but forfeit their life? Or what will they give in return for their life?

Matthew 16:26

The bottom line is a phrase that comes up often in different contexts. It comes originally out of the world of business accounts. After the day's selling and the multiplications, additions, subtractions, percentages, and inventories are all calculated, the bottom line shows a single fact: profit or loss. Did I make money today or lose it? Is this business in the red or in the black?

Many things take place in the course of a business day—courtesies, pleasures, obligations—but if no profit shows up on the bottom line, the business, as a business, *fails*. Jesus uses this accountant's language that all of us know so well to train us in evaluating our lives. There is a similarity between running a business and living our lives: the bottom line shows whether it is done well or badly.

There is also a contrast: the bottom line in business shows how much you accumulate, but the bottom line in life shows how much you give away.

Place of Worship, Place of Witness

It is a perverse misunderstanding of the act of worship to suppose that it is voluntary. It is not voluntary; it is required. True, it is not coerced. Some churches have tried to force Christians to church by threatening them with hell if they didn't go or bribing them with blessings if they did. But coercion is no attribute of God.

We reject all attempts at legislating or manipulating church attendance. But because the Holy Spirit does not make personal visitations on Sunday morning to those of us who are feeling a little lazy or think we have something more important to do and twist our arms to get us to the place of worship, we must not suppose it is up to us to do as we please in these matters. Why? Because the place of worship is a place of witness—a witness that God speaks to us and that we are ready to listen, a witness that God changes people and that we are changed by his action, a witness that God gives himself to us so that we may live and gladly receive his gift.

Many people don't know that God is here speaking and saving and giving himself. They think God is remote. They think God is silent. They think God is a nice idea at times of crisis. They don't know that God is right now speaking and changing lives and pouring out abundant life. They need to know it. Your witness is required.

When you walk into a house of worship and take your place—singing, praying, listening, receiving—you are a witness to this action of God, the greatest of all actions in the world.

You are irreplaceable in this witness. No one has your particular slant on it. No one has your way of seeing it and saying it—*being* it. If there are two hundred others there and you are absent, the two hundred can't replace your witness, for you are unique. Your witness is required.

I want our churches to be saturated with the joy and spirit of evangelism, letting the world know how good God is and how accessible he is to each man and woman, child and youth. There are many ways that the spirit of evangelism gets expressed, but it all begins in the act of worship. If you are not there, you detract from what we are doing together. You also diminish your credibility as a person of obedient and biblical faith.

I know you don't feel essential when you walk through church doors, greet a few people, sit in a pew, and sing and pray. But it is essential. Your witness is required.

Our Witness Is Required

Christ is here. There can be little doubt about that. The whole world (not quite, but it seems like it) has acknowledged his arrival, and even those who don't believe in him have been glad to make money off him once a year at Christmas.

But something is required of us beyond mere acknowledgment. Our witness is required. We must realize afresh, deep in our hearts, that this event, this coming of God in Jesus to us, is the center of all history. It is the center of the eternal meaning of each of our lives. But then the telephone begins to ring again. The urgencies of our jobs demand our attention. Our priorities pull us in different directions.

But Christ is not an occasional happy thought! His presence is not greeting-card inspiration or a monetary pickup. It is the blood-and-bone reality of our everyday lives.

And to this we must bear witness. There are so many who don't know it. They know *about* it, but they don't *know* it. They have access to the *information* but have not the first idea of the glorious *experience*. And we ourselves get distracted, preoccupied with meeting the demands of those around us.

But we who have been given this great gift of faith and have free access to this incomparable act of worship are required to give witness—to say, in words and actions, what is going on here on this third planet from the sun.

On Sabbath

Time is holy. But how often do you hear anyone say so? More likely you hear, "Time is money." And time, like money, is something that you mostly feel you don't have enough of, *ever*. On occasion, when you have time in which nothing is scheduled, you will "kill time."

Odd, isn't it? We have more leisure hours per person per year as a country than anyone could have guessed a century or two ago. But we are not leisurely. We are not relaxed. We are anxious. We are in a hurry. Anxiety and hurry ruin intimacy and sabotage our best intentions in faith, hope, and love—the three actions in which most of us set out to do our best.

Sabbath comes from the Hebrew word for *stop*. It's a stop sign on the street of days. Stop what you are doing and look around; see what is going on. And listen.

Sabbath is the biblical tool for protecting time against desecration. It is the rhythmic setting apart of one day each week for praying and playing—the two activities for which we don't get paid but that are necessary for a blessed life. Blessed lives are what we are biblically promised. A blessed life is not a mere survival life but a bountiful one. Praying and playing are warp and woof, woven in the bounty.

That is why I want you to keep a Sabbath. I want you to live well. I want you to live whole and mature, with appreciation and pleasure, experiencing the heights and depths of God's glory in your bodies and your work, your friends and your gardens, your minds and your emotions, at the ocean and in the mountains. You can't do that if you are on the run. You can't do that if you are watching the clock.

What is going on when we rest? *God,* mostly—God creating, God saving, God providing, God blessing, and God speaking. God does us the great honor of inviting us in as coworkers in his genesis work. We participate in the creating, saving, providing, blessing, and speaking. It is good work. When we do it well, we are exhilarated. When we do it badly, we are bored. The world of work, a powerful field of energy, demands a great deal of *us.*

But in the midst of the work, we can easily lose touch with the origin of our work and its purpose, the place of our work and its rhythms. Instead of feeling the creativity of work, we become compulsive. Instead of feeling the freedom and dignity of work, we feel trapped and demeaned. And so at the end of each workweek, God calls a Sabbath: *stop.*

So we stop. Our work—our lives—opens into freedom, into leisured goodness, into God-ness. There is something basically godlike about work, so when we are at work, it is easy to assume that we are gods, making things happen, in charge, managing lives and materials, indispensable to the cosmos. But although our work is godlike, we are not gods. We have a higher calling in life than as tinhorn, local gods: we are called to be humans who explore the fullness of freedom and who experience the relationships of love. We can't do that if we don't stop working long enough to see ourselves in relation to God's work, stop what we are doing so that we can take a long, attentive look at what God is doing, stop what we are saying so that we can take in what God is saying. *Sabbath.*

In expectation, we seek to "life up" others with our hope. Turn to a friend who is discouraged, or find a neighbor who is disheartened. Use your hands and speech to invite that friend or neighbor into a life of purpose and hope. Will we live in a selfish panic, pushing and grabbing, fearful that we won't get our share? Or will we live openly and generously, helping others to receive God's gifts and welcome his love? The expectant command is for us to *encourage*.

The church should work to continually clarify and celebrate God's coming to us. Our lives and worship should fan the fires of expectation.

How to Keep a Sabbath

Keeping the Sabbath is easy: we pray and we play, two things we were pretty good at as children and can always pick up again with a little encouragement.

Praying is our great act of freedom in relation to heaven. This is the exercise of our bodies and minds in acts of adoration and commitment, practices of supplication and praise, and ventures of forgiving and giving. We explore the source of our freedom in Christ's crucifixion and resurrection, enjoy it, and share it when we assemble for worship.

Then there is playing. This is the great act of freedom in relation to earth. We exercise our bodies and minds in games and walks, in amusement and reading, in visiting and picnicking, in puttering and writing. We take in the colors and shapes, the sounds and smells. We let the creativity of the creation nudge us into creativity. We surprise ourselves by creating a meal or a conversation or an appreciation or some laughter that wasn't in our job descriptions. We have some fun.

So, if it is so easy, why do we find it so hard? Because the world is out to steal our Sabbath—to dilute it, to fragment it, and to eliminate it. The "world" is sometimes our friends, sometimes our families, and sometimes our employers. They naturally enough want us to work for them, not waste time with God, not be our original selves. If the world can get rid of our Sabbaths, it has us to itself. What it does with us when it gets us is not very attractive: after a few years of Sabbath breaking, we are passive consumers of expensive trash and anxious hurriers after trash pleasures.

We lose our God and our dignity at about the same time. That is why I want you to keep a Sabbath. Guard the day. Protect the leisure for praying and playing. Unlike Christians in earlier generations, we get no help from our culture in keeping the Sabbath. But blaming the culture is no excuse. We can, though, help each other by praying together each Sunday in the name of Jesus, who taught us to pray, and playing in honor of Christ.

On Praying and Playing

Praying and playing are often connected in the Christian imagination. What playing is to the body, praying is to the spirit. Or you can start from the other end: what praying is to the spirit, playing is to the body.

Both involve a kind of frolic and exuberance, a delightful splashing around. They both show us off at our best: spontaneous, intense, exploring dimensions of our lives that are obscured or ignored in the press of getting through our chores or carrying out job assignments. Another likeness is that what children do with seeming naturalness—pray and play—adults have to make time for or even make a special effort to engage in. But when we do, we sense that in praying and playing, we become more ourselves, not less, living more in the image of God, living more truly in touch with family, friends, self, and the world.

God, Our Center and Circumference

When we choose to worship with the people of God, we affirm that God is center and circumference to our lives.

The act of worship builds our inner foundations and nurtures the eternal relationships we practice all the hours and days of the week.

As we sing and pray, give and listen, we participate in what French philosopher Jacques Maritain has said that our modern world most needs:

> New fire, the essential renewal . . . an inner renewal. . . . It consists of a change of attitude, or a displacement of values that takes place in the deepest recesses of the soul, and has to do, first of all and essentially, not with any way of acting or externally behaving . . . but with a way of seeing them before God, and a way of loving them better.*

---

* Jacques Maritain, *The Peasant of the Garonne: An Old Layman Questions Himself About the Present Time,* trans. Michael Cuddihy and Elizabeth Hughes (Eugene, OR: Wipf and Stock, 2011), 72.

Invitation, Not Manipulation

The spirit of worship, the personal integrity of our responses, is preserved by always announcing worship as an invitation, not a command. The call to worship goes out regularly and repeatedly, as the church knows that it is absolutely essential, one of the foundational acts of Christian existence. But it also knows that personal relationships cannot be coerced, so however necessary worship is, it cannot be forced. And so you are called to worship, not commanded.

Being at worship has no value if you are not here to worship. The component parts of worship have no value in themselves. The best-ordered service of worship in the world, the most skillfully preached sermon, the most exquisite singing—none of it causes a flicker of interest in almighty God. God is spirit: personally alive, seen to be in relationship with us in our aliveness.

And so we don't force people into a sanctuary. We don't coerce. We don't manipulate, putting on emotional pressure. We don't offer inducements, promising a little extra zing in their lives if they go to church, raising expectations for unworthy ends. And we don't play on their guilt, trying to arouse a sense of obligation so they won't let the old team down or disappoint the pastor.

We simply *invite*. We do so patiently and persistently, as the church has invited the people for nearly two thousand years, gathering them to listen to hear again that God loves us, that he forgives us, that he has a way of salvation for us, and encouraging the faith that responds in praise and commitment.

PART FOUR

On Mercies

GOD's loyal love couldn't have run
  out,
  his merciful love couldn't have
  dried up.
They're created new every morning.
  How great your faithfulness!
I'm sticking with GOD (I say it over
  and over).
  He's all I've got left.

Lamentations 3:23–24, MSG

Beneath the Surface

Lift up your heads, O gates!
   and be lifted up, O ancient doors!
   that the King of glory may come in.

Psalm 24:7

We live too much on the surface. All of us do.

Our culture, in conspiracy with the devil, does everything it can to keep us preoccupied with things like making sure the images we see in our mirrors are acceptable, getting across the street without being hit by a car, and keeping food on our tables and gasoline in our cars.

With only peripheral murmurs of dissent, the dominant voices say, "Consume! Hurry! Buy! Don't think! Don't be quiet! And, above all, don't pray (except in emergencies)." We must develop strength for swimming against the stream of the culture. Seasons of prayer and fasting, such as the yearly discipline of Lent, amplify those good murmurs of dissent that do speak against the louder messages.

Listening, we give our attention to Jesus and dive into the depths, exploring freshly the reality beneath the surface, the wonderfully complex reality of God's image formed in us, of Christ's salvation worked out in us. We listen to the countercultural words of dissent now in stereo: "Deny yourself! Slow down! Live! Think! And, above all, *pray.*"

Prayer is our best way of getting to the heart of our experience and realizing how it can be used by our Lord in this grand enterprise that we all signed up for when we acknowledged Christ and became part of making a kingdom of God.

We lift our heads to meet the King.

The Root Rightness

Why is there so much joy in the world? Why do people laugh? Why do people smile? What accounts for all the celebrations? We read the newspapers, only to learn that most things are going wrong most of the time. We consult our own hearts and find that anxiety, guilt, and doubt intrude on the best of days. Yet joy keeps erupting in and around us. Maybe the newspapers don't tell the whole story. Maybe our own hearts don't give the whole truth. Maybe something right is going on in life. Maybe something basically good and affirmative has happened and is happening and the smiles and laughter and celebrations are evidence of it.

God is in action in our lives. God's will is being worked out in our history and in our hearts, and that will is salvation. This is the center fact in our existence, and that people laugh and smile and celebrate is evidence of it. Even the people who don't know it or don't believe it have to live in a world where God is doing his great work. They, too, often not knowing why, smile and laugh and celebrate, witnessing despite themselves to the foundational affirmations, the root rightness.

Voice in the Action

Go od does not impose right solutions on us. God does not pull strings behind the scenes to engineer his will despite what we are doing and saying. He treats us with dignity, giving us the freedom to be in on what he does, to have a voice in the process. Prayer is our voices in the action of God. It is also God's voice in the actions of people.

The God Who Comes to Us

G od comes. He is not an object at the center of the universe. He is not a fixed point on an astronomer's map of heaven. He is active and moving—and this movement has *direction*. He comes to us.

God doesn't wander around, window-shopping from galaxy to galaxy, juggling the moons of Jupiter and casually admiring the rings of Saturn. We are his destination. And he didn't simply come once and then return to spend the rest of eternity, like an old tourist, telling stories of his trip and boring angels with slides of his visit. He came. He comes. He will come again.

We know what to expect when he comes and comes again, because we know exactly what happened when he came to us in Jesus. And Jesus, at his ascension, promised that he would come again. The Christian life is lived between those two comings: he came, and he will come.

To believe and serve a God who comes, to live lives in a world to which God comes—what does that mean? This is the expectant believer's task: to clarify that question, to celebrate it, and to live heartily and hopefully in response to the God who comes to us. Will we live slovenly, with unbuttoned minds and disheveled spirits, thoughtlessly supposing that the same things will be forever monotonously repeated, over and over again, in creation and history? Or will we live alertly and ardently, convinced that God continues to come to us and will come to us again in Jesus? Will we believe that in expectantly waiting for his coming, being hospitable to his arrival, we are getting the most out of life?

Creation and Becoming

The Genesis Week of creation is matched by the Gospel Week (or Holy Week) that describes our salvation. The seven days of genesis display the external environment in which we live—this amazing world of light and water, soil and plants, fish and birds, and animals and humans. The gospel days—the seven days between Palm and Easter Sundays—tell the story of events that get inside us, that shape our salvation. The genesis days provide a framework for our lives; the gospel days provide meaning and purpose for them. Both weeks are holy.

The splendor of the Christian way is its integration of these two weeks' energies. We see those energies harmonized and complete in Jesus, the Christ. As we remember and worship him, our lives are reformed around the basic patterns of our existence and we are renewed from the center. In Jesus, we become more our original genesis selves. At the same time, we become *more* than ourselves—we are being made gospel creatures in Jesus.

Such attention sharpens our perceptions of where we have come from and where we are going, who we are, and who we are becoming.

New Life and Holy Luck

The new life Christ inaugurates in this world and in our lives is a breath of fresh air: full of surprises and spilling out spontaneities.

Still, it is easy to miss its genius. It is so *different,* so counter to our accustomed ways of doing things, that we readily relapse into business as usual. We begin to view the gospel as an occasional interlude in our dreary routines but not practical in the workday world.

But God did not go to all the trouble of bringing Jesus to us merely to provide us with diversion. The Nativity was not a nightclub act. Christian experience is not a trip to a religious Disneyland to provide us with a store of anecdotes and wonders to tell our friends back home.

We are lucky to be saved, incredibly lucky, but it is holy luck. This isn't the luck of being momentarily *exempt* from disaster or tedium. This is a different kind of luck—holy luck—that *invades* disaster and tedium. And so, even while we are still exclaiming over the wonders and marveling at the glory, Jesus carefully and painstakingly shows us how the new life is embedded in the common life.

A Different Freedom

In all nations, there are people who live out a freedom that is both different and better than that claimed by their fellow citizens, whether capitalist or communist or anything in between. These people call themselves *Christians*.

Their freedom has a two-thousand-year-old tradition. It has been enjoyed by people under every kind of political system, in all kinds of cultures, and in the face of diverse social and economic realities. They call their freedom "freedom in Christ." These Christians trace the origin of their freedom to a revolution set in motion by Jesus Christ. The Word that Christ speaks to us sets us free; the praise we offer develops freedom; the prayers we offer make freedom possible for others.

As people faithful in worship and attentive to God's Word, we will witness to that freedom. We will be free, but not with the world's freedom. We will be *Christians*.

The Appointment

We all have had well-intentioned (if somewhat vague) plans to do something nice for another person. "Love your neighbor" (Matthew 22:39) is a command we all plan on obeying . . . *sometime*.

For many of us, it never amounts to more than a sentimental daydream, but for others, this fuzzy benevolence gets real. It becomes a simple, unpretentious, focused act of love that leads to health, to hope, to salvation for an actual person. The general, dreamy desire to help out in some way or another becomes a specific, creative act of compassion. A person walks out on the gossipy discussion of all that is wrong with the world and all that needs to be done in the world, finds another who needs help, and keeps the holy appointment she did not know she had.

On Connections

One of the great excitements of the first Christians was simply the discovery of *connections*—connections that joined God and the personal. This faith was not one of secret mysteries or hidden doctrines. It met one's life. It mattered.

Faith is the experience of connecting causes with effects, heaven with earth, the invisible with the visible. And it invites questions: Are we connected or disconnected? Is what we know about God connected with what we know about ourselves? Is what we experience at work connected with what we experience in worship?

It is still exciting to discover the connection between praying the Lord's Prayer and consulting a lawyer, between reading the stock-market quotes and reading the Bible, and between opening a hymnal in church and turning the control knob of the car radio.

This is because every truth about God is at the same time a truth about *ourselves*.

On Pentecost and Dry Bones

The sheer volume and quality of wreckage in the world and culture around us are appalling: wrecked bodies, wrecked marriages, wrecked careers, wrecked plans, wrecked families, wrecked alliances, wrecked friendships, wrecked prosperity.

We avert our eyes. We try not to dwell on it. We wake up expecting health and love, justice and success. We try to keep our hopes up. And then some kind of crash puts us or someone we care about in a pile of wreckage. Newspapers document the ruins in photographs and headlines. Our own hearts and diaries fill in the details. Are any promises, any hopes, exempt from the general carnage? It doesn't seem so.

Why, then, is not every intelligent and awake person a cynic? Why does not the wise person despair? Is it sheer naivete that keeps people striving for the best, investing themselves in acts of compassion, giving themselves sacrificially to add to the available beauty, and suffering abuse to witness to the truth?

Why? Because of Pentecost. Because the Holy Spirit is among us and within us. Because God's Spirit continues to hover over the chaos of the world's evil and our sin and shapes a new creation and new creatures. Pentecost means that God is not a spectator, in turn amused and alarmed at world history; rather, he is a participant. Pentecost means that the invisible is more important than the visible, at any single moment and at any single event that we choose to examine. Pentecost means that everything, especially everything that looks to us like wreckage, is material that God is using to make a praising life.

The prophet Ezekiel saw a field of dry bones: dismembered skeletons whitened under the pitiless Babylonian sun. Every one of those bones had once been part of a laughing and dancing child, an adult who made love and plans, or a believer who had voiced doubts and sung praises in the sanctuary . . . and sinned.

The dry bones were all that was left. Sin and judgment on the sin were the last word—at least, that was what it looked like. That is always what it looks like. Ezekiel thought so, and everyone with eyes to see and a brain to think thought so.

But Pentecost claims another last word. Pentecost celebrates the coming together of the bones into connected, sinewed, muscled human beings who speak and sing and laugh and work and believe and bless their God. It happened, and it happens. It happened in Israel, and it happens in church. You can see it happen most any time and most any place in the world. You can see it happening and be part of the happening.

Pentecost celebrates the great fact that through the Holy Spirit, God puts us together again as praising people, no longer dismembered but remembered into the resurrection body of Christ, which we believe includes the people of God.

Celebrate this and live more deeply into the action of God.

All

I can do all things through him who strengthens me.

Philippians 4:13

When we are unsure of ourselves, we exaggerate. We compensate for inadequacy by braggadocio. Fearful that people will drift away from the dull stories of our lives, we put on a little verbal polish to hold their attention. Knowing how often we do this, we assume others do it also, and so we learn to suspect all big words of masking some emptiness.

Paul often used big words. Was he overstating? Was he stretching the truth? But his style shows otherwise—no frenzy or shouting. His subject simply exceeds his vocabulary. In the final sentences of this most exuberant of his letters, a quite astounding statement is made but is embedded in a syntax of matter-of-factness. It is hyperbole by understatement: "I can do all things through him who strengthens me."

All documents a solid maturity. Immaturity is the stage between innocence and experience, when we think that by changing what we have or who we are with or where we are, we can arrange contentment. Maturity is life developed inwardly, knowing that the significant acts are our responses. There is a great deal we can do nothing about: weather, other people's emotions and attitudes, and economic conditions. But there is one way we can do much: offer up the centers of our lives in acts of love and faith, risking our beings in relationship with God.

That becomes an *all* that suffuses life with contented strength.

A Serious Interruption

The church is characterized as a community of people who must take God seriously.

Now, be careful as you listen. I'm not saying that the church is that group of people who take God seriously. Sometimes we don't. There are many of us who go for long times without taking God seriously. What I am saying is that the church is that group of people who *must* take God seriously. We can't go very long without being interrupted, because God is going to interrupt us.

God won't let us get by with our religious lives very long on our own terms. He keeps invading and keeps interrupting.

The Manner of Our Master

In all matters of ministry, Jesus is our master. We apprentice ourselves to him so that we might become skilled and mature and wise, for ministry involves doing what Christ did, speaking what Christ commands, praying in the name of Christ—and getting *good* at it.

Ministry is not some vague impulse to do good. It is not a generalized desire to help others. It is not a mystic hand-holding with all those who are groping toward the infinite. It is learning to do what Christ did and learning to do it in the *way* that he did it: acting and speaking and praying after the manner of our master.

Interdependences

Economically and physically, we are caught in a great web of interdependences. Spiritually, this is even more so. The church is the most complete expression of all these interdependences. It is an expression of them in terms of God's grace—a grace that surrounds us and moves through us as people created to enjoy (and depend on) the praise of his glory.

The Ministry of Things

"No ideas but in things"* was the dogma of one our best poets, William Carlos Williams. At a time in our American history when sentimental ideas and fluttering emotions were thought by many to be superior instances of culture—purer forms of reality than, say, cracks in the sidewalks and broken benches in an unkempt park—Williams took a red wheelbarrow in a barnyard and some bits of broken green glass in a hospital courtyard and used them to make us participants in the reality of everyday existence. He knew that the vocation of the poet is not to embroider life with sentiment, not to entertain people with lullaby rhythms, and not to instruct us with easily remembered moral rhymes.

The poet's vocation is to get rid of lies and illusions and evasions so that we can live firsthandedly, seeing and smelling and touching and breathing the reality of existence for ourselves and then loving or hating it, blessing or cursing it—whatever we wish—but no longer indifferent to it or insulated from it. In this, poets are brothers and sisters to the ministry of the Word and sacraments. And, in fact, in earlier times, the poet and the priest were often the same person.

No part of creation can be bypassed in the life of faith. None of it is an inconvenience to be put up with. None of it is a stumbling block intruded by the devil to trip the feet of those whose eyes are piously lifted in praise to God. Creation is made

---

* William Carlos Williams, "Paterson," Poetry Nook, www.poetrynook.com/poem /paterson-0.

by God as a structure for meeting God. Sacrament means that the external and internal are parts of the same reality. Creation and redemption proceed from the same God. Our bodies and souls are sustained by what God makes in creation and gives in redemption.

The moment Jesus picked up something, it became obvious just by the way he handled it that it was something *good*. It was a piece of God's creation and therefore a means for meeting God: jugs of water at Cana, the sound of the wind in Jerusalem, waves of the Galilean sea, the paralytic's pallet at the Bethesda pool, the corpse of Lazarus, and his own flesh and blood.* *Things*.

Things cannot be bypassed. They are essential.

The sacraments of the church are material means that God uses to bring us grace. God uses the stuff of creation to bring us into relationship with himself. Jesus is the master sacramentalist. He used anything at hand to bring us into awareness of God and into response to God.

At the table in the Upper Room, training the Twelve in a ministry of sacrament, Jesus had usable materials ready—wine and bread—for they were sitting that night at a Passover table. They planned to eat the Passover there soon or had just eaten it. Three of the gospel writers describe how Jesus took what he found on the table and used it to make a sacrament that we now call the Lord's Supper and how he commanded us to continue to celebrate it using his words and acts. We have continued to do it. We will do it again tonight. But John skips that part of the story about the bread and wine. He omits the solemn, precise words of institution and the prayer of blessing and tells us that while they were sitting around this table, Jesus got a bucket of soapy water and began washing the feet of his friends. When he

---

* See John 2:1–11; Acts 2:1–4; Matthew 8:23–27; John 5:1-18; John 11; Hebrews 2:14.

finished, he told them that they were to do it too (see John 13:1–17).

It was the kind of thing that Jesus characteristically did. He took unlikely things and used them in surprising ways to bring the people around him into encounters with God. Things are holy. But because of indolence or fatigue or selfishness or ignorance or rebellion—that is, because of our sin—we forget this or are unaware of it or feel separated from it. We feel neglected or perhaps alienated. We feel unclean. We think that if we had better-looking bodies, we might be more conscious of being made in the image of God. We think that if we lived in more comfortable surroundings, we would be in better positions to experience the comfort of the Holy Spirit. We are sure that if our feet weren't so dirty and the day weren't so hot, we would feel more like loving our neighbors. Jesus, sensing all this, grabbed a bucket of water, threw a bar of soap into it, took a towel made out of an old feed sack, and washed the feet of the disciples. Bucket, feet, towel, water—sacramental elements.

A ministry of sacrament is responsible for announcing and demonstrating that the world is holy, as opposed to, say, useful or beautiful or profane or mean. A ministry of sacrament insists on the holiness in the sick body, in the lonely heart, in dirty feet, in polluted streams, in a depersonalized institution, in vineyards, in wheat fields—and then involves us in meeting God there. The baptismal font and the communion chalice are the boundaries between which we discover that no part of this material world is unusable by God and that every part of it is created to be good, a vital part in the machinery of salvation.

Jesus trains us in a sacramental ministry so that we live and love and believe—and teach others to live and love and believe—in the presence of God mediated through this-worldly realities.

Jesus washing the feet of his friends. The Master kneeling

before the disciples. Soapy water, dirty feet. And this on a stage set for the world's salvation. Jerusalem, remember, was at that moment full of the sounds of Passover: the bleating of sacrificial lambs, the singing of the hallelujah psalms, prayers for the Messiah to come, sighs too deep for words, songs of hope and joy. The city was electric with rumors of Jesus, who acted with commanding authority and whose words arrested and revealed.

Only by learning a ministry of sacrament, of the sacredness present in the real stuff of life, are we saved from our own egos, from our own feelings, from confusing an elevation in our temperatures with the fire of the Holy Spirit. In this, we can minister *like* Jesus, not merely *for* him.

Wreaths and Wheels

There was a centuries-old practice among the Christians who lived far north and who learned to integrate the rhythms of the weather with the truths of our faith. They did not separate secular and religious—nature and gospel were the outside and inside of the same reality.

As the days grew shorter and colder and it looked as though the sun were leaving for good, they brought all ordinary actions and daily routines to a halt. They gave in to the nature of winter and came away from their fields and put away their tools. They removed the wheels from their carts and wagons, festooned them with greens and lights, and brought them indoors to hang in their halls. They brought the wheels indoors as a sign of a different time, a time to stop and turn inward. They wooed the light and warmth: Christ, the light of the world.

Imagine what would happen if we were to be as literal as our ancestors and remove just one tire—say, just the right front one—from the family Pontiac and use this for our Advent wreath. Indeed, things would stop! Our daily routines would come to a halt. We would have the leisure to incubate. We could attend to the precarious pregnancy of the season and look after ourselves. Having to stay put, we wouldn't be able to dilute our expectant hope of Christ born in us with a distracting run to town.

What would it mean for us to deepen our expectancy in this way? What might we gain from knowing the seasons, from learning the wisdom of losing a wheel once in a while?

On Our Connection
with the Whole Church

O ne of the things we mean when we say in our creed that
we believe in the *catholic** church is that there is more to
church than what we see and hear in our congregations. We
believe that what God is doing here in us he is also doing in
many other places among many other people and that none of
us is complete apart from everyone else.

Catholic, then, means "the whole church," separated in
time and space into congregations but joined by the Spirit in
common faith and purpose. All Christian churches are organically connected. If we could see and hear this in its entirety—
complex and intricate, vast and mighty—it would astound us.

---

* Eugene is referring to the entire community of Christians throughout history
and the world, not specifically to the Roman Catholic tradition.

Toward a Good End

Pause for a moment and think about this: we Christians are the result of something that started two thousand years ago, and the results are not only all over the globe but also *here,* right where you are now. Impressive.

But impressive as it is—the long continuity, the undiminished energy, and the staggering numbers—it can also be misleading. Religious activity as such can mask spiritual lethargy. Religious words can lose their spiritual integrity. Religious identities can become social roles. The term *Christian* in Lebanon, for instance, carries a different set of meanings than it does here.

So we stay vigilant. A good beginning does not ensure a good end. We return to worship to stay alert to the living God and take precaution against self-deceit.

To grow inwardly demands far more of us than to grow outwardly. Whatever is happening with Christianity around the world, this question still remains for us: Are we ourselves larger, our lives bigger, and our spirits livelier?

PART FIVE

On Glories

Because Jesus was raised from the dead, we've been given a brand-new life and have everything to live for, including a future in heaven—and the future starts now! God is keeping careful watch over us and the future. The Day is coming when you'll have it all—life healed and whole.

1 Peter 1:3–5, MSG

Resurrection Groundwork

His master commended the dishonest manager because he
had acted shrewdly; for the children of this age are more
shrewd in dealing with their own generation than are the
children of light.

Luke 16:8

Jesus tells some strange stories. We scratch our heads—
"What on earth is he saying to us?" He does not make
things plain. He teases our minds, our spirits. We wonder and
ponder.

Jesus was not what today is called a good communicator,
the kind of person whom advertising firms hire to write copy.
This is because, as it turns out, Jesus is primarily interested not
in communication but rather in communion. His chief concern
is not that we get a new piece of information but that we become new people. And to do that, he needs to get us *involved*—
asking questions, wondering who we are and where we stand,
curious and intrigued, on tiptoe, ready to take risks.

The Resurrection Pivot

We need to draw a sharp line between religious consumerism and a gracious gospel. The line is blurred and even erased by the world and by our sin. Resurrection draws the line bold and distinct again, dividing a consumer religion from a gracious gospel.

A consumer religion shops for God in the religious shopping malls and tries on the latest fashions. A gracious gospel discovers us in our ignorant waywardness and invites us into the membership of Christ. Many people are living on the wrong side of the Resurrection, trying to get something interesting or useful for their lives from God rather than letting him do something gracious and eternal for them. Five verbs distinguish the Resurrection pivot: *believe, sacrifice, abide, love,* and *sanctify.*

Resurrection is the pivot point. Up to the event of the Resurrection, we are consumers of religion, looking for what we can get out of God. After the Resurrection, we are surprised by amazing grace and given what we weren't even looking for, what we didn't even know we needed.

Consumer religion is a shopping spree in the boutiques of idolatry as we try to raise our standards of meaning or "purchase" some angelic protection. A gracious gospel is God's gift—a life that we didn't know was possible for us.

Resurrection life marks the difference. It is both more wonderful and more difficult than consumer religion. It is more wonderful because it is God's inventive creation, perfectly customized to our condition. It is more difficult because God is in charge and we would rather be in charge. It is, after all, our life—or so we feel.

We counter the difficulty and embrace the wonder by a simple practice of faithfulness. Week after week, year after year, we return to this Easter pivot, to the remembering of the Resurrection, seeking to discard our consumer habits and receive the gifts of grace. We work to pay attention to the verbs of the Resurrection, God's actions in Christ that turn life around for us. We practice our participation in their actions, for we are convinced that our lives, as well as Christ's life, turn on the pivot of God's resurrection action.

On the Consuming Fire

> In the fire of his passion
>   the whole earth shall be consumed.
>
>   Zephaniah 1:18

I recall two pictures of the use of fire from my youth in Montana. My father was a butcher, and I often was with him on cattle ranches, examining and buying cattle. Sometimes when a field had grown up heavy with weeds and thistles, a rancher would set fire to it. Men would be carefully ranged all around the area so the fire would not get out of control. Then some gasoline would be poured to give a good start, a match would be tossed, and several acres would be covered with fire.* Soon it would be black and empty. The fire had done its work, cleared the weeds and thistles so they wouldn't seed and spread to other fields. The fire of God is like that. It comes to us in judgment to purge out what displeases, what makes it impossible to receive the companionship of Jesus.

Another use of fire that was particularly vivid came at cattle-branding time. Iron brands were thrust into the fire and left until they were red hot. Nothing was destroyed in those brands, for they were already tested and hard. All the fire did to

---

* To state the very obvious, please do not try this risky fire-starting method for yourself based on Eugene's anecdote.

them was intensify their effectiveness so that when pressed to the hide of the young calves, they quickly left their marks.

God's judgment is like fire as it comes to our lives. It purges, burns out all that is useless and bad in our lives. And then it brings the part that is good, that is his image in us, to a white heat of effectiveness in his service so that, like a branding iron, we can leave his mark on whatever we touch. God's judgment is not always pleasant. As Zephaniah said, it may be "a day of distress and anguish" (1:15). But we must remember that it is a judgment of *preparation*—getting us ready for an eternity of association with him who comes to us.

Vistas of the Holy

The Christian faith by any accounting, even by those who do not embrace it, has to do with things vast and splendid: breathtaking vistas of the holy, awesome insights into the human, prodigious commands, and bright blessings.

The sheer extravagance of the gospel dazzles us. But it also, at the same time, intimidates us. Aware of our ordinariness, we disqualify ourselves from membership in such extraordinary company. We admire from afar, but in our everydayness, we don't really think that we have the right stuff for living the big questions and the grand encounters. Many of us fail to live the fullness of the faith not because we don't believe it but because we don't feel up to it. At such times, we don't need strong arguments to persuade us of the truth. We need simple directions to guide us into participation.

Imitation is our simple instruction. The way we get in on the splendors of grace is not by mastering elaborate theological dissertations or by practicing austere, ascetic regimens; it is by joining up with others in the way of faith. Regular, deliberate association with friends who agree that knowing Christ is the goal is something anybody can do.

All of us have one impressive accomplishment to our credit that is not unlike, in its own way, living the gospel: we learned to speak our native language fluently. For many of us, this is English. It is a difficult language. The syntax is bewilderingly intricate. Yet, by the age of five or so, all of us had mastered it—and without even going to school. How did we do it? Our parents and brothers and sisters and friends simply began talking, and we began imitating. We just hung around the people who were doing it, and before long we were doing it too. We "learn" Christ the same way: by hanging around the people who are doing it.

This imitation works for individuals. It can also work for cultures. Historically, a primary means of expansion of the Roman Empire was not by military conquest but by colonies. People weren't forced to be Romans; they were shown how to be Romans by a group of people who simply lived among them and did it. A colony in the times of the Bible was a group of people who set down in a foreign place and did everything they did in the Roman way. The purpose of the colony was not to separate itself from the population to preserve itself inviolate but to demonstrate and establish a so-called civilized life in a so-called barbarian land.

Christians set down to live the common life, much as everyone else does, except that we do it Christ's way. The primary means of expansion of the "civilization" of God in a "barbarian" world is not by lecturing people in the truth or coercing them to be good. It is by establishing communities of imitation, worshipping congregations where we simply live the common life—but in God's way.

Lazarus in the Spring

> Jesus said to her, "I am the resurrection and the life. Those who believe in me, even though they die, will live, and everyone who lives and believes in me will never die. Do you believe this?" She said to him, "Yes, Lord, I believe."
>
> John 11:25–27

Lazarus died. Jesus brought him back to life. Why did he do it? We don't know. He did it. It was the kind of thing he does. There is no particular reason. Jesus doesn't give reasons—he gives life.

Lazarus was an actual person, with weight, height, and birth date. He had parents. He had two sisters, with whom he played as a child and probably fought, as brothers and sisters usually do. From where he lived, he could look to the south and see, six miles away, the town where Jesus was born. When he looked to the west, a mile or so across a valley, he could see the city of David and its temple. He grew up and got a job. One day he met Jesus. They became good friends.

And then he died. Everybody does it eventually. We are born and we live and we die. We have a birth date and will have a death date. Between the two dates, we grow up and play with our friends, learn the names of the streets we live on and the towns we live in, and get jobs. We meet people. With some of them, we become friends. Then we die. That's it.

Except. Except for Lazarus. Lazarus lived again. The definitive word on Lazarus was neither his birth date nor his death date but his *life* date. Jesus called him to life again. His two sisters thought his life was over and there was nothing to do but reminisce over the old times. His family and friends were mistaken. They were mistaken because they thought death was the final word and it wasn't. Life was the final word.

Why did Jesus do that? Why did he call Lazarus back from the tomb and set him before his sisters and friends alive? He didn't do that for everyone—why make an exception with Lazarus? Maybe to surprise us with life at the very moment we think death is the last word. Birth is no surprise, nor is death, but *life*—life when we think the story is over, life when we think family and friends and job are played out—is always a surprise.

Not all life, or at least what we call life, is a surprise. A lot of it is dead: predictable and boring and embalmed. But every life Jesus calls into being is a surprise. And every time it happens, like each daffodil that pushes through its leaf-mat shroud, it is an exception. Like Lazarus. Like you when Jesus speaks your name in scripture and sermon and sacrament.

Read again the story of Lazarus. Detach yourself from the world's dead predictabilities, the "winter of our sins," and immerse yourself in the life-making words of Jesus that make exception, like each year's spring, from death to life in each of us, one by one.

The Water or the Wave?

I do not consider that I have made it my own; but this one thing I do: forgetting what lies behind and straining forward to what lies ahead.

Philippians 3:13

We badly distort what it means to be a human being if we think about life only in terms of solving problems or accomplishing tasks. In the areas in which we are most ourselves, life doesn't work like that.

An athlete, for instance, does not solve the problem of hitting a baseball by hitting a home run. It is not a task he does and is then finished with, simply spending the rest of his life replaying a video of the great moment. To be an athlete means going out to play every day, using the body not just to hit home runs from time to time but to play the game.

A lover does not solve the problem of marriage by celebrating an anniversary of a good year together, then going on to something else, merely pausing occasionally in the midst of other preoccupations to look at the anniversary pictures. Lovers keep learning new ways to love—new ways to put their emotions, their imaginations, and their bodies into the act of love.

An adolescent doesn't solve the problem of growing up simply by arriving at the age of twenty-one and then insisting on being treated as an adult by announcing to everyone the incontrovertible evidence of her birth certificate.

And we don't solve the problem of life by getting right with God, merely circling the date of our conversion on the calendar, and giving testimony to our faith. There is an incredibly rich world of grace and mercy to explore. To paraphrase, Paul said, "I do not *consider*" (and that word for consider, *logizomai,* means "to look over the scene and assess it") "and I can hardly be said to have made a start."

"But this one thing I do"—*one thing.* Paul was echoing Jesus's words to Mary and Martha. Mary was sitting at Jesus's feet in listening love while Martha was hurrying through the house, tidying up and getting a meal ready, and Martha complained about Mary: "Why isn't she helping?" Jesus spoke the integrating words: "Martha, Martha, you are anxious and troubled about many things; one thing is needful. Mary has chosen the good portion, which shall not be taken away from her" (Luke 10:41–42, RSV).

Good Company

On Halloween, while children in our neighborhoods dress up as spooks, others of us anticipate the next morning: All Saints' Day. It is an opportunity for us Christians to remember and pray in continuity with our ancestors, to be blessed by what they gave us, and to be challenged to continue in the way of the Cross. Some of these may be close ancestors (parents, grandparents, and other family members); others are distant (biblical ancestors, Christian saints, and men and women we have admired and been influenced by). In our prayers to God and remembrance of their witness, we often find that they are nearer than we had thought and realize how much we continue to be shaped by them. Good company!

The company we keep shapes the kind of people we are. We are *known* by the company we keep. Christian company is the best: exuberant, sane, worldwide, centuries deep. Christian company comprises not only the people we invite into our homes, the people we worship with, and our allies in mission and witness but also our ancestors. We characteristically cultivate relationships with our predecessors in this pilgrim way so their wisdom can become our wisdom, their love continue in our affections, and their faith be linked to our discipleship.

A Good Death

The phrase *good death* is not used often in our current culture. But until about a hundred years ago, all pastoral practice was directed toward preparing people for it—for living in the expectation of a good death.

But instead of embracing the holy opportunity of our mortality, a secular culture tries to insulate us from the experience of death. But can it? No. Death is one of the elemental mysteries of our existence. Still, our culture succeeds to an astounding degree. Considering the frequency and inevitability of death, it is astonishing how well we are able to avoid and deny its reality.

But that avoidance diminishes us.

Resurrection Detectives

As yet they did not understand the scripture, that he must rise from the dead. Then the disciples returned to their homes.

John 20:9–10

There is a lot we don't know. There are days, many of them, when we don't know what is going on. Events tumble out randomly, it seems. Is there rhyme or reason? Sometimes we think there must be; other times we throw up our hands in puzzlement. There are days when the world is bright with meaning and every bird and flower a witness to the glory; we dance and sing with the innocence of animals. But those days are then snatched by the starless nights when the dark has seeped into our souls and we cower in fear and despair, pulling the covers over our heads.

A tomb, hewn out of a rocky hillside, had been emptied of its corpse. Two men stood in front of it, puzzled. What was going on here? Not only was the body gone from the tomb, but the meaning was gone from their lives. The corpse had a name: Jesus. Alive, he had convinced the two men that their lives had purpose, that it was worthwhile to live, that everything fit together in a design of salvation, and that love was possible. In the days they had spent with him, they had become convinced that life was wonderful and that God was good. Then they saw him killed and buried. It was a terrible loss, a smashing disappointment. But we do survive these things: death, separation, and loss. They also would survive. They had wonderful memories. His tomb would mark the best they had ever known. Every time they visited it, they would go over the experiences and be grateful and try their best to live well, worthy of his love and friendship.

But now the tomb was empty. The living Jesus was gone; the dead Jesus was gone also. Reality was turning somersaults on them. Nothing was nailed down. They were in the middle of a mystery. The mystery, as mysteries sometimes do, turned them into detectives. They spotted a clue. They used their heads. They followed the clue. And it led them to resurrection.

There are clues everywhere, still. It is up to the curious to pick them up, follow them, make the correct deductions from them, and live before the mystery of life in a believing faith.

Upward, Undiminishing

I press on toward the goal for the prize of the upward call
of God in Christ Jesus.

Philippians 3:14, RSV

We will badly miss Paul's meaning in these words if we
think or suppose that he is an energetic, aggressive go-
getter, hell-bent to get everything there is out of life. Many people are like this, straining forward: "I press on . . ." The great
questions are, What are they after? What is the goal? What is
the prize that they are so bent on getting?

It is here we must give our attention: "the upward call of
God in Christ Jesus." Here is an emphasis that we ought to be
getting used to by now if we have spent much time in Scripture.
God has done the decisive act in Jesus Christ. God calls us. He
calls us to be his; he calls us to be in relation to him; he calls us
to know him. The upward call is not the call to make the most
of ourselves, to get the most out of life, and to give it the old
college try. We are talking not about a task but about *faith*.
Paul is announcing not a career development but a personal
call.

This is in contrast to the other calls that come to us, as we
are called to be many things and do many things. Much of our
lives can be described by the ways those calls determine our
actions, but they never include who we are—only what we can

do. We are called to do certain kinds of work, to be workers, consumers.

If I do only what you want me to do, there is too much of me left out. If you do only what I want you to do, there is too much of you left out, for the demands that are made on me come from the needs of others. Many of them are legitimate. Many of them are necessary for me to respond to. But if that is all I am, I am not myself. God calls me not because of what he wants to get out of me but because of what he wants me to get out of him. His call is the only one that does not diminish me.

Again, *his call does not diminish me*. His call does not distract me from my essential being but confirms it. His call does not diminish my core identity.

His call establishes it.

Now you've got my feet on the life path,
      all radiant from the shining of your face.
Ever since you took my hand,
      I'm on the right way.

Psalm 16:11, MSG

ABOUT THE AUTHOR

EUGENE H. PETERSON, translator of *The Message* Bible, wrote more than thirty books, including *Every Step an Arrival*, *As Kingfishers Catch Fire*, *Run with the Horses*, and *A Long Obedience in the Same Direction*. He earned a degree in philosophy from Seattle Pacific University, a graduate degree in theology from New York Theological Seminary, and a master's degree in Semitic languages from Johns Hopkins University. He also received several honorary doctoral degrees. He was founding pastor of Christ Our King Presbyterian Church in Bel Air, Maryland, where he and his wife, Jan, served for twenty-nine years. Peterson held the title of professor emeritus of spiritual theology at Regent College, British Columbia, from 1998 until his death in 2018.

ABOUT THE TYPE

This book was set in Sabon, a typeface designed by the well-known German typographer Jan Tschichold (1902–74). Sabon's design is based upon the original letter forms of sixteenth-century French type designer Claude Garamond and was created specifically to be used for three sources: foundry type for hand composition, Linotype, and Monotype. Tschichold named his typeface for the famous Frankfurt typefounder Jacques Sabon (c. 1520–80).